Philly by the Numbers

From 00-99: the greatest Philly sports legends to wear each jersey number

Michael Egenolf

This book is dedicated to my wife Susan and my son Ian for their love, support, and patience while I spent countless hours typing, researching, and being otherwise disengaged from family activity. I am grateful for your continued support.

I love you both!

A thank you to Christian and April, both of whom read sections of this book and offered excellent suggestions.

To my family and friends, and the legions of die-hard Philly sports fans that have co-commiserated, cried, yelled, cheered, and celebrated like only die-hard Philly fans know how, this labor of love is for you!

M. E.

I would like to acknowledge several research outlets that have been instrumental in my quest to compile the information contained herein. Any mistakes are my own.

Mlb.com/Phillies

Philadelphiaeagles.com

NHL.com/Flyers

NBA.com/Sixers

Baseball-Reference.com

Pro-Football-Reference.com

Hockey-Reference.com

Basketball-Reference.com

Wikipedia.com

Philly by the

Numbers

Table of Contents

45 –	Tug McGraw
	Terry Mulholland
	Tim Hauck
46 –	Herman Edwards
	Jon Dorenbos
	Ryan Madson
	Kevin Gross
47 –	Larry Andersen
48 –	Wes Hopkins
	Daniel Briere
49 –	Jose Mesa
	Tommy Greene
50 –	Jamie Moyer
	Guy Morriss
	Steve Mix
	Randall Cobb
51 –	Carlos Ruiz
	Reggie Wilkes
	William Thomas
52 –	Ricky Bottalico
53 –	Hugh Douglas
	Bobby Abreu
	Shayne Gostisbehere
	Nigel Bradham
	Ken Giles
	Darryl Dawkins
54 –	Brad Lidge
	Jeremiah Trotter
	Lucious Jackson
55 –	Dikembe Mutombo
	Brandon Graham
	Frank LeMaster
56 –	Jerry Robinson
	Byron Evans
	Joe Blanton
	Chris Long
57 –	Bill Cowher
58 –	Trent Cole
	Ike Reese
	Jordan Hicks
	Jonathan Papelbon
59 –	Seth Joyner
60 –	Chuck Bednarik
61 –	Wayne Gomes
	Steve Everitt
	Stefan Wisniewski
62 –	Jason Kelce
63 –	Ron Baker
	Jake Diekman
64 –	Ed Blaine
65 –	Lane Johnson
	Charlie Johnson
66 –	Bill Bergey
	Yanick Dupre
67 –	Jamaal Jackson

68 –	Jaromir Jagr
69 –	Jon Runyan
	Evan Mathis
70 –	Al Wistert
71 –	Jason Peters
	Ken Clarke
72 –	Tra Thomas
	Wade Key
73 –	Shawn Andrews
	Ed Khayat
74 –	Mike Pitts
75 –	Stan Walters
76 –	Jerry Sisemore
	Bob Brown
	Shawn Bradley
77 –	Paul Coffey
78 –	Carl Hairston
	Hollis Thomas
	Marion Campbell
79 –	Todd Herremans
	Brandon Brooks
80 –	Cris Carter
	Irving Fryar
81 –	Terrell Owens
82 –	Mike Quick
	LJ Smith
83 –	Vince Papale
84 –	Keith Krepfle
	Freddie Mitchell
85 –	Charles Smith
86 –	Fred Barnett
	Zach Ertz
	Charle Young
87 –	Brent Celek
	Donald Brashear
88 –	Eric Lindros
	Keith Jackson
	John Spagnola
89 –	Calvin Williams
	Chad Lewis
90 –	Corey Simon
91 –	Fletcher Cox
	Andy Harmon
92 –	Reggie White
93 –	Jake Voracek
	Jevon Kearse
94 –	Ndukwe Dike "N.D." Kalu
95 –	William Fuller
	John Bunting
	Mychal Kendricks

96 –	Clyde Simmons
	Bennie Logan
	Derek Barnett
97 –	Jeremy Roenick
	Rhett Hall
	Darwin Walker
98 –	Connor Barwin
	Greg Brown
	Mike Patterson
99 –	Jerome Brown
100 –	Wilt's 100

Phillies Hot Corner

Eagles Eyrie

Flyers Face Off Circle

Sixers Net Effect

Phifty Philly Phirsts

What's in a Name

Brotherly Love in the City of Brotherly Love

50 from Philly

And the Award goes to…

Philly's Greatest Voices…

Put Me In, Coach!

PHILLY BY THE NUMBERS

Fifty Years of Philadelphia Sports 1967-2017

In One Era and Out the Other

Philadelphia has always been a city passionate about its sports teams. Through highs and lows, year after year, we, the Philly faithful, cheer our teams on, regardless of how painful that may be.

Nineteen hundred and seventy two, a memorable year indeed. The Godfather dominated at the box office, Fiddler on the Roof, A Clockwork Orange, and Cabaret were among the year's best films. All In the Family was the #1 TV show in America. Nights in White Satin by the Moody Blues, Roundabout by Yes, and American Pie by Don McLean took over the radio waves.

1972, the year of the Rat, was also the year Pong, Grease, Ziggy Stardust, ABBA, and HBO's debut. The year the Miami Dolphins went 17-0. The year Richard Nixon kept the White House by taking 49 of 50 states in the election. The year the world was introduced to the Atkins Diet. It was also the year terrorists murdered 11 members of the Israeli Olympic team at the Munich Olympics.

While we watched that tragedy unfold on our TV sets each night, Steve Carlton, in his first season with the Phillies, was quickly making everyone forget about Rick Wise. Carlton would go on to win 27 games and his first Cy Young Award in 1972. Carlton won 27 of the Phillies 59 wins. A truly remarkable feat. It was the city's only sports bright spot that year.

While the Oakland A's were winning the World Series, the Dolphins were perfect, the Lakers were the toast of the NBA, and the Boston Bruins were hoisting the Stanley Cup, Philadelphia sports was mired in historic futility. Sports in Philly in 1972 was the worst sports year for any North American city.

Ever.

Anywhere.

43 years later Philadelphia did it again. In 2015, Philadelphia's winning percentage wasn't as bad as 1972, but at .375 for its four teams, it was a very close second.

Furthermore, with the end of the Sixer's season in May 2017, Philadelphia finished with its worst three-year run ever. The futility was staggering. Collectively, 2014-2016/17 was mind-blowingly awful.

There are twelve cities* in the US represented by teams in MLB, NFL, NHL, and NBA. Of those twelve cities, four of them had all four teams make the playoffs over that 2014-2016/17 span. Three of the twelve cities have won championships in those three years. Two cities have done it twice.

	City	# of teams	# of playoff trips	# of Champs	Winning Seasons	Winning %
1	Washington	4	8*		10/12	.572
2	Boston	4	8*	2	8/12	.534
3	Chicago	5	7	2	7/15	.524
4	Los Angeles	7	11		12/19	.523
5	Dallas	4	7*		7/12	.515
6	Detroit	4	6*		6/12	.495
7	Miami	4	3		3/12	.484
8	New York City	8	8		10/24	.466
9	Minneapolis	4	4		4/12	.435
10	Denver	4	2	1	3/12	.433
11	Phoenix	4	2		2/12	.407
12	Philadelphia	4	1		1/12	.389

WASHINGTON (Nationals, Redskins, Captials, Wizards), BOSTON (Red Sox, New England Patriots, Bruins, Celtics), CHICAGO (Cubs, White Sox, Bears, Black Hawks, Bulls), LOS ANGELES (Dodgers, Angels, Rams, Kings, Anaheim Ducks, Lakers, Clippers), DALLAS (Texas Rangers, Cowboys, Stars, Mavericks), DETROIT (Tigers, Lions, Red Wings, Pistons), MIAMI (Marlins, Dolphins, Florida Panthers, Heat), NEW YORK (Mets, Yankees, Giants, Jets, Rangers, New Jersey Devils, Knicks, Brooklyn Nets), MINNEAPOLIS (Minnesota Twins, Minnesota Vikings, Minnesota Wild, Minnesota Timberwolves), DENVER (Colorado Rockies, Broncos, Colorado Avalanche, Nuggets), PHOENIX (Arizona Diamondbacks, Arizona Cardinals, Arizona Coyotes, Suns), PHILADELPHIA (Phillies, Eagles, Flyers, Sixers)

-NHL records are figured in wins and losses. Overtime losses and shootout losses may get you a point in the standings, but here, they are still losses and are calculated as such.

– Los Angeles is part of the twelve because the Rams played in LA in 2016.

* - all teams made playoff appearance

So as you can see, Philadelphia sports teams over those three seasons have won less than four out of every ten games. Four teams, three years, 12 seasons... one playoff series and one winning season.

But Philly has enjoyed some highs as well. Philadelphia had a nice run after the abysmal 1972 season. The Flyers would win back-to-back Stanley Cups just a few years later. The Phillies in 1980 and the Sixers in 1983 would win championships.

In fact, in 1980, all four teams competed in their league's championship. It's the only time it has ever happened. That we went 1-3 was a bit painful. But the Phillies parade down Broad Street was glorious. 1980 was a year of excitement and magical sports moments. The Flyers incredible 35-game unbeaten streak, Pete Rose catching the ball that popped out of Bob Boone's glove in game six and Tug McGraw striking out Kansas City Royals Willie Wilson to win the World Series, and Wilbert Montgomery rushing for 194 yards against Dallas to lead the Eagles to their first Super Bowl appearance.

Will Philadelphia once again enjoy greatness after enduring such futility?

There is cause for optimism in the City of Brotherly Love. The Eagles improbable run to their Super Bowl LII championship has ignited the fire in Philly sports once again. The Flyers and Sixers followed up the Eagles championship with playoff appearances of their own. And the Phillies look to be headed down that road, as well.

For the 2017-18 season, three of the four Philly teams made the postseason. That's three times as many as the previous 3 years combined.

Will Aaron Nola and Rhys Hoskins bring the Phillies back to power?

Will Joel Embiid and Ben Simmons be a championship slam-dunk?

Can Ivan Provorov, Shayne Gostisbehere, Nolan Patrick, and Carter Hart net us a Cup and bring Lord Stanley back to Broad Street?

Can Carson Wentz, Fletcher Cox, and the rest of the Eagles soar to another Super Bowl?

The future is now. Things could get very interesting very quickly.

Either way, as Philly sports fans, we will endure. We will cheer, paint our faces, redefine the term tailgating, yell, scream, ingest copious amounts of antacids, and live and die with our teams.

From the fanatical fan to the dauntless diehard and all of Philly's faithful, this book is for you.

Philly by the Numbers is a collection of the best we have witnessed in our teams. It's a celebration of the greatest moments, memories, and heroes of our beloved teams.

In writing this book, I had to set some guidelines. I chose to focus on the last 50 years of Philly sports as opposed to highlighting on the same page a player from the 1980's and 1880's. However, I also did not want to simply ignore some of our greatest just because they played in a different era. So players who've had their numbers retired, regardless of the era they played, are included. Secondly, I kept this within the realm of our four major sports teams in the four major sports leagues. Who knows, maybe a future version will include soccer, indoor football, lacrosse, etc.

The Philadelphia Athletics and Philadelphia Warriors (as well as the pre-Sixers Syracuse Nationals), are included in greatest moments that would be unjust to leave out.

Please visit us at Phillybythenumbers.com to post comments, criticisms, suggestions, and your favorite stories or memories.

Without further ado, I present Philly by the Numbers. Enjoy!

Michael Egenolf

April 27th, 2018

Bernie Parent – Blazers (1972-73) NHL Hall of Famer Bernie Parent wore "00" as a member of the WHA Philadelphia Blazers during the 1972-73 hockey season. The following season Parent led the Philadelphia Flyers to their first Stanley Cup win. While the Blazers are not one of Philly's BIG FOUR major sports franchises, Parent brought Philly two Stanley Cups and he's in the Hockey Hall of Fame, so his "00" as a Blazer makes the list!

Did you know...

... Omar Olivares of the Philadelphia Phillies was the first player of Philly's BIG FOUR to wear "00". In case you are wondering who he is, he pitched 10 innings for the Phillies in 1995.

... No Flyer and no Eagle has ever worn "00". Rick White of the Phillies (2006), Eric Montross (1998), Benoit Benjamin (1998-99), Amal McCaskill (2004), and Spencer Hawes (2011-14) of the Sixers are the only other players to wear "00" in Philly major sports history.

0

Did you know… No Flyer and no Eagle has ever worn "0". Al Oliver of the Phillies (1984), Orlando Woolridge (1994), Alvin Jones (2002), Jeremy Pargo (2013), Darius Johnson-Odom (2014), Brandon Davies (2015), Isaiah Canaan (2015-16), Jerryd Bayless (2017-18) of the Sixers are the only other players to wear "0" in Philly major sports history.

Even up…

0… Number of times Wilt Chamberlain fouled out in his Hall of Fame NBA career.

0… Eagles points scored in their Lincoln Financial Field debut, a 17-0 loss to the Tampa Bay Buccaneers on September 8th, 2003.

0… Number of points the Eagles gave up in their first two championship-winning games. On December 19, 1948 in blizzard-like conditions, the Eagles defeated the Chicago Cardinals 7-0 at Shibe Park in Philadelphia. On December 18, 1949, in a soaking downpour, the Eagles defeated the Los Angeles Rams 14-0 at the Los Angeles Memorial Coliseum.

1

Bernie Parent – Flyers/Goalie (1967-71, 1973-79) Widely regarded as one of the all-time best goaltenders in NHL history, Bernie Parent put together back-to-back seasons in 1973-74 and 1974-75 that earned him two Vezina Trophies (best goaltender) and two Conn Smythe Trophies (playoff MVP), and was instrumental in the Flyers winning their only two Stanley Cups to date. Parent had two stints with the orange and black, 1967-68 to 1970-71 and 1973-74 to 1978-79. An accidental high stick struck Parent's right eye through the mask opening and ended his career. Parent was a five-time NHL All Star and was inducted into the Hockey HOF in 1984. The Flyers retired Parent's #1 on October 11th, 1979 and inducted him into the team's HOF in 1988.

Richie Ashburn – Phillies/CF (1948-1959) was one of the most beloved figures in Philadelphia sports history. Whitey was a career .308 hitter, a six-time NL All Star, two-time NL Batting champ, and in 1995 was inducted into Cooperstown. Ashburn joined the Phillies Wall of Fame in 1979. The Phillies retired Ashburn's #1 and honored him by naming the entertainment area at Citizens Bank Park "Ashburn Alley". Ashburn was part of the Phillies broadcast team from 1963 until his death in 1997.

Did you know...

... Eagles Super Bowl XV barefoot kicker Tony Franklin kicked a 59-yard FG in Dallas on November 12th, 1979. At the time, it was 4th longest in NFL history.

... Sixers Michael Carter-Williams won the NBA Rookie of the Year honors in 2013. He also had an NBA rookie-debut record 9 steals in his first game in the NBA.

... Sixers Samuel Dalembert doesn't use milk with his cereal. He uses orange juice.

2

Mark Howe – Flyers/D (1982-1992) Son of hockey legend Gordie Howe, Mark was a four-time NHL All Star, a four-time Barry Ashbee Award winner, a three-time Norris Trophy finalist, and an Olympic Silver Medalist with USA Hockey at the 1972 Winter Olympics in Sapporo Japan. Howe had his #2 retired by the Flyers and was inducted into the Flyers HOF in 2001, the US Hockey HOF in 2003 and the Hockey HOF in 2011.

David Akers – Eagles/K (1999-2010) David Akers was simply the greatest placekicker in Eagles history. Akers, a six-time Pro Bowler holds the NFL record for points in a season with 166. He also holds the NFL record for most field goals in a season, with 44. Akers holds 6 other NFL records. Akers played more games in an Eagles uniform than any other player in team history (188). Akers was a member of the Eagles Super Bowl XXXIX team. Akers hit an NFL-record 17 FGs of 40 yards or longer and led the league with a 40.8 yard FG average during the Eagles 2004 march to the Super Bowl. Akers was inducted into the Eagles Hall of Fame in 2017, the first kicker so honored.

Moses Malone – Sixers/C (1982-1986) Moses Malone was a dominant NBA rebounder earning him the nickname "Chairman of the Boards." He was the NBA MVP and NBA Finals MVP in 1983 helping the Sixers capture their

3rd NBA Title in franchise history. The twelve-time NBA All Star was inducted into the Basketball Hall of Fame in 2001.

Bob Dailey – Flyers/D (1976-77 to 1981-82) Bob "the Count" Dailey was a two-time NHL All Star and two-time Barry Ashbee Award winner. For the first half of his NHL career, "the Count" at 6'5" was the NHL's tallest player. Dailey scored a career-high 21 goals during the 1977-78 season, his first full season with the Flyers. Dailey played on the Flyers record-breaking 35-game unbeaten team, and scored 17 postseason points during the Flyers 1980 Stanley Cup Finals run. Dailey fractured his ankle in a collision with Buffalo Sabres Tony McKegney battling for an icing call on November 1st, 1981 in a Flyers 6-2 loss. The injury effectively ended "the Count's" career at age 28. Bob Dailey passed away in 2016 after a long battle with cancer.

Ed Van Impe – Flyers/D (1967-68 to 1975-76). Ed Van Impe was the second captain in Flyers team history, wearing the "C" from 1968-1972. Van Impe was Calder Trophy (Rookie of the Year) runner-up (Bobby Orr) the year before the Flyers selected him from the Chicago Black Hawks in the NHL Expansion Draft. Van Impe played on both Flyers Stanley Cup championship teams. The gritty Van Impe once took a puck in the mouth, lost 6 teeth, and took 50 stitches to his lips and tongue... then finished the game. Van Impe is famous for his crushing check on Soviet Red Army winger Valeri Kharlamov during Super Series '76 that led to the Soviets leaving the ice in protest. The three-time NHL All Star was inducted into the Flyers HOF in 1993.

Did you know...

... Flyers defenseman Mark Howe was inducted into the Hockey Hall of Fame in 2011 joining his legendary father Gordie Howe. They were just the 4th father-son duo enshrined as players in NHL history (Bobby and Brett Hull, Lynn and Lester Patrick, and Earl and Oliver Seibert).

Even up...

2... Stanley Cups won by the Flyers in team history. The 1st in 1973-74 defeating the Boston Bruins 4 games to 2, and repeating as champs in 1974-75 defeating the Buffalo Sabres 4 games to 2.

2... World Series Championships for the Phillies in team history. The 1st in 1980 defeating the Kansas City Royals 4 games to 2, and the 2nd in 2008 defeating the Tampa Bay Rays 4 games to 1. The 2008 Series vs Tampa Bay featured the only game in World Series history completed two days after it began.

3

Allen Iverson – Sixers/G (1996-2006, 2009-10) One of the most exciting players in a generation, Iverson, the 1997 Rookie of the Year, led the Sixers to the NBA Finals in 2001 as the league's MVP. The four-time NBA Scoring Champ was an eleven-time NBA All Star, winning the All Star Game MVP in 2001 and 2005. A.I. is the Sixers all-time leader in three-pointers with 885. The Sixers retired Iverson's #3 in 2016. Iverson was nicknamed "The Answer" by a family friend as he was about to attend Georgetown University. In May, 2002 The Answer "answered" his critics with a twenty-two expletive rant with the famous line "We're talkin' 'bout practice."

Tom Bladon – Flyers/D (1974-1978) The two-time All Star Flyer blueliner had the game of all games for NHL defensemen when on December 11, 1977 "Boomer" Bladon scored four goals and assisted on four others in an 11-2 romp over the Cleveland Barons. It was the first hat trick ever for a Flyers defenseman, and his +10 is the highest single game plus/minus in NHL history. During the following off season Bladon, along with Orest Kindrachuk and Ross Lonsberry, was traded to the Pittsburgh Penguins for the sixth overall pick in the draft (and an 8th rounder). That 6th overall pick turned out to be another of the best Flyers to ever wear #3, Behn Wilson.

Behn Wilson – Flyers/D (1978-83) Hard-hitting and offensively gifted Behn Wilson was the sixth overall player taken in the 1978 NHL Entry Draft. Wilson made the team right out of camp and appeared in all 80 games that season for the orange and black. His 49 points and 197 PIMs set Flyers rookie defensemen records. Wilson was a 1981 NHL All Star and finished that season with 63 pts, 237 PIMs (6th) and an impressive +41 (tied for 9th w/Gretzky). Following the 1982-83 season, big #3 was traded to the Chicago Black Hawks for another #3, Doug Crossman, and a 2nd round pick (Scott Mellanby).

Did you know…

… On April 20th, 2003, Allen Iverson scored 55 points in a post-season game against the New Orleans Hornets. It's tied (Rick Barry, Michael Jordan) for the 2nd most points in an NBA post-season game (Charles Barkley 56 w/Phoenix Suns).

… Phillies catcher Todd Pratt hit a two-run walk-off homer against the Boston Red Sox in a 6-5 Phillies win in 13 innings. Phillies broadcaster Scott Graham's call of the June 21st, 2003 game-winning homer has been immortalized in a talking bottle opener.

… Flyers D Dan McGillis is the brother of actress Kelly McGillis (Top Gun, Witness).

Oddly enough...

3... The number of times Phillies all-time HR leader (548) Mike Schmidt was NL MVP (1981, '82, '86).

3... Super Bowl appearances for the Eagles in team history. The Eagles lost to the Oakland Raiders in 1980, lost to the New England Patriots in 2004, and defeated the New England Patriots in 2018 for their first ever Super Bowl Championship.

4

Dolph Schayes – Sixers/C-F (and Syracuse Nationals) 1949-50 to 1963-64. Dolph Schayes was inducted into the Naismith Memorial Basketball Hall of Fame in 1973. Schayes played his entire 15-yr career with the Sixers/Nationals franchise. Schayes was a player-coach for the Sixers and was NBA Coach of the Year in 1966. Selected by the NBA as one of the league's all-time top 50 players for the NBA's 50th Anniversary in 1996. The twelve-time NBA All Star had his number retired by the Sixers in 2016.

Barry Ashbee – Flyers/D (1971-74) Barry Ashbee won a Stanley Cup with the Flyers as a player (1973-74) and as an assistant coach (1974-75). In 1973-74 Ashbee was named a 2nd team NHL All Star, was 4th in Norris Trophy voting, and was a team high +52 for the season way ahead of runner-up Bobby Clarke (+35). Ashbee's playing career ended that year during the playoffs when he took a puck to the eye off the stick of Dale Rolfe of the New York Rangers. Ashbee spent the next three years as a Flyers assistant coach. Near the end of the 1976-77 season, Ashbee was diagnosed with Leukemia. He died a month later on May 12, 1977. The Flyers retired Ashbee's #4 and annually award the Barry Ashbee Trophy to the Flyers best defenseman as voted by a panel of local sportswriters.

Lenny Dykstra/CF – Phillies (1989-1996) Three-time NL All Star, Dykstra was the spark plug that ignited Macho Row and the 1993 pennant-winning Phillies. "Nails" was NL MVP runner-up (Barry Bonds) in 1993. Dykstra batted .348 against the Toronto Blue Jays in the World Series hitting four homers in the series loss. Dykstra's post-baseball life has been a rollercoaster of highs and lows as detailed in his 2016 memoir, *House of Nails: A Memoir of Life on the Edge.*

Jake Elliott – Eagles/PK (2017-Present) Jake Elliott kicked a game-winning 61-yard FG vs NY Giants on September 24th, 2017. It was the longest NFL FG ever kicked in Philly, the longest in Eagles team history, and the longest ever by an NFL rookie. His 53-yarder vs Atlanta Falcons on January 13th, 2018 is the longest FG by a rookie in the NFL playoffs. His 46-yarder vs NE Patriots in Super Bowl LII is the longest FG by a rookie in a Super Bowl. His 5 FGs of 50+ yards during the 2017 season is also a team record. Elliott started the year on the Bengals practice squad but was picked up by the Birds after week 1 when Caleb Sturgis went down with a season-ending injury. Elliott was the Bird's Special Teams MVP for 2017.

Did you know...

... On May 6th, 1991, Phillies Lenny Dykstra and Darren Daulton were seriously injured in a car accident after leaving John Kruk's bachelor party.

... Phillies Lenny Dykstra's uncle Tony Leswick scored a game-seven overtime Stanley Cup-winning goal for the Detroit Red Wings over the Montreal Canadiens in 1953-54.

... On August 23rd, 2009, in a 9-7 win over the New York Mets, Phillies 2B Eric Bruntlett had an unassisted triple play in the 9th inning. He caught a Jeff Francoeur line drive, stepped on second base and then tagged the runner coming from 1B. It was just the 15th unassisted triple play of the modern era.

... Flyers Barry Ashbee was once suspended by the NHL for 8 games for punching referee Bryan Lewis in the nose in a 5-3 Flyers win over the Pittsburgh Penguins on January 27th, 1973.

Even up...

4... consecutive shutouts for Phillies pitchers in 1969 (Jerry Johnson, Woody Fryman, Larry Jackson, and Rick Wise)

4... Cy Young Awards for Steve Carlton 1972, '77, '80, '82

4... NHL-record goals in a period, Tim Kerr 4/13/85 (T/with 12)

4 – OT goals by Shayne Gostisbehere in 2015-16 season, an NHL rookie record.

5

Donovan McNabb – Eagles/QB (1999-2009) The number two overall draft pick in 1999 out of Syracuse, McNabb led the Eagles to five conference championship games (2001, 2002, 2003, 2004, 2008) and a Super Bowl XXXIX appearance (2004). The six-time Pro Bowler is the Eagles career passing leader (32,837 yards), completions leader (2,801), and TD pass leader (216). The NFL's 6th most prolific rushing Quarterback (3,469 yards) had his #5 retired by the Eagles and was inducted into the Eagles Hall of Fame in 2013. And remember, "5" will always love you.

Pat Burrell – Phillies/OF (2001-2008) Pat the Bat was selected by the Phillies 1st overall in the 1998 amateur draft. Burrell is 4th on the Phillies all time HR list with 251. He hit 20 or more homers in eight consecutive seasons. In 2002 Burrell became just the 12th player in team history with 30 HR's and 100 RBI's in a season, finishing with 37 HR's and 116 RBI's. Burrell entered the Phillies Wall of Fame in 2015 and was a member of the Phillies 2008 World Series Champions.

Did you know...

... Flyers defenseman Kim Johnsson, winner of the Barry Ashbee Award in 2002 and 2004 was acquired from the New York Rangers along with Jan Hlavac and Pavel Brendl when the Flyers sent Eric Lindros to the Rangers on August 20th, 2001.

... Donovan McNabb was sacked an NFL record 12 times in a 16-3 loss to the NY Giants on 9/30/07

... Pat Burrell had the last base hit at Veterans Stadium on September 28th, 2003. Burrell's bottom of the 9th single was followed by Chase Utley hitting into a double play ending the Veterans Stadium chapter of Phillies history.

... Eagles QB Roman Gabriel appeared in the John Wayne movie "The Undefeated."

Oddly enough...

5... 1st round draft picks from USC by the Eagles in the NFL Draft, more than any other college (Nelson Agholor 2015, Mike Patterson 2005, Charle Young 1973, Tim Rossovich 1968, and Leo Riggs 1946).

5... goals in a playoff game by Flyers Reggie Leach vs Boston Bruins on May 6th, 1976, for an NHL record (tied w/ 4 others).

5... points (2 goals - 3 assists) in an NHL debut for Flyers Al Hill vs St. Louis Blues on February 14th, 1977. It's an NHL Record for points in an NHL Debut. Hill got into a fight with Blues Bob McMillan for the only debut Gordie Howe hat trick in NHL history.

6

Julius Erving – Sixers/F (1976-1987) Dr. J was one of the most exciting and gifted players to ever wear an NBA Uniform. Erving was inducted into the Basketball Hall of Fame in 1993 and his uniform #6 was retired by Sixers in 1988. Erving was an NBA All Star for every year of his Sixers career. He was league MVP in 1983 leading the Sixers to their NBA Championship. In 1994, Sports Illustrated Magazine named Dr. J as one of the 40 most important athletes of all time.

Ryan Howard – Phillies/1B (2004-16) Ryan Howard was a three-time NL All Star and was NL MVP in 2006. The "Big Piece" twice led the NL in HR's (2006, '08) and was a three-time RBI leader (2006, '08, '09). Howard also won the NL Rookie of the Year in 2005. The Big Piece was truly a big piece of the Phils 2008 World Series Championship. Howard was the fastest in MLB history to reach both 100 HR's and 200 HR's. He is the first player in Phillies history to knock 50 HR's in a single season hitting 58 in 2006. His 85 HR's in his first 1,000 AB's is also an MLB record.

Andre Dupont – Flyers/D (1972-80) Andre Dupont played seven and a half seasons for the Flyers, twice scoring double-digit goals. He is best known for his slap shot from the point that was deflected by Rick MacLeish in game 6 of the 1973-74 Stanley Cup series against the Boston Bruins. Dupont assisted on the only goal of the game and the Flyers were

Stanley Cup Champs. Dupont thought he'd scored the goal and "Moose" did the Dupont Shuffle in celebration.

Chris Therien – Flyers/D (1994-2004, 2005-06) Chris Therien played more games on defense for the orange and black than any other player in team history (753). "Bundy" is best known for his uncanny ability to shut down Jaromir Jagr, one of the games' most explosive wingers. Therien won a silver medal in 1994 with Team Canada at the XVII Olympic Winter Games in Lillehammer, Norway. Therien has been part of the Flyers broadcast team since 2008.

Did you know...

... Phillies catcher Tim McCarver scored the last run at Connie Mack Stadium scoring on an Oscar Gamble walk-off RBI single in the 10th inning vs Montreal Expos on October 1st 1970.

... Flyers defenseman Wayne Hillman (1970-73) made his NHL debut with the Chicago Black Hawks on April 16th, 1961. The Black Hawks just happened to win the Stanley Cup that night. Wayne Hillman is the only NHL player to have his name inscribed on the Stanley Cup after playing just one game.

Even up...

6... The Flyers have lost their last 6 Stanley Cup Finals appearances in a row. After winning back-to-back Stanley Cups in 1974 and 1975, the Flyers lost to the Montreal Canadiens in 1976, the New York Islanders in 1980, the Edmonton Oilers in 1985 and 1987, the Detroit Red Wings in 1997, and the Chicago Black Hawks in 2010.

6 – The Eagles have drafted 6 players from both Oregon and USC since the 2000 NFL Draft, the most of any college.

7

Bill Barber – Flyers/LW (1973-84) Barber was drafted 7th overall in the 1972 NHL Entry Draft. He was runner-up for the Calder Trophy as Rookie of the Year in 1973. His 420 goals are the most in a Flyers jersey. As a member of the famed LCB line, Barber was a huge part of the Flyers winning back-to-back Stanley Cups. Barber appeared in 4 Stanley Cup Finals with the orange and black. Barber was a 50-goal scorer in 1975-76 when he finished with 116 points. The Flyers retired Barber's #7 in 1990, and he was inducted into the Hockey Hall of Fame the same year. Barber was the 5th Captain and 14th Head Coach in team history and is the only player to serve in both capacities over their Flyers career. Barber won the Jack Adams Award as NHL Coach of the Year for the Flyers in 2000-01.

Ron Jaworski – Eagles/QB (1977-86) Jaworski is one of the greatest quarterbacks in team history. He led the Eagles to a 1980 Super Bowl appearance vs. Oakland Raiders. He was named NFC Player of the Year and was a Pro Bowler that same season. The Polish Rifle holds the NFL Record for longest pass play, a 99 yarder to Mike Quick vs. Atlanta Falcons on November 10th, 1985 (tied w/ others). Nicknamed "Jaws" by Sixer Doug Collins prior to the 1980 Super Bowl, Jaworski was added to the Eagles Honor Roll in 1992.

Did you know...

... In 2001, Defensive Coordinator Jim Johnson's defense became just the 4th team defense in NFL history to hold opponents to 21 points or less in every game of a complete 16-game season.

... Eagles QB Michael Vick was the 50th Eagles starting QB in team history.

Oddly enough...

7... The number of points the Eagles scored to win their first NFL Championship, defeating the Chicago Cardinals 7-0 on December 19th, 1948 in blizzard-like conditions. It was also the first-ever televised championship game.

7... The Flyers have been awarded 7 penalty shots against the New Jersey Devils. They only scored one (11/3/2011 Max Talbot on Johan Hedberg).

8

Mark Recchi – Flyers/RW (1991-92 to 1994-95 and 1998-99 to 2003-04)
Rex holds the Flyers all-time record for points in a season with 123 in
1992-93. He played two separate stints with the orange and black. His
only 50-goal season of his 17-year career came in the 1992-93 season
when Recchi potted 53 for the Flyers. Recchi won the Bobby Clarke
award three times, (1993, 2000, and 2004), the Yanick Dupre Award
(1992-93), and the Toyota Cup in 2004. During the 2009-2010 playoffs
Recchi became the 3rd oldest player in NHL history (Gordie Howe, Chris
Chelios) to score a playoff goal, and also was the oldest player in NHL
history to score twice in a playoff game, doing so against his old team the
Flyers in a 5-4 OT loss. A seven-time All Star (3 with the Flyers), Recchi
was inducted into the Hockey Hall of Fame in 2017.

Bob Boone – Phillies/C (1972-1981) Bob Boone, a standout defensive
catcher, played ten seasons in Phillies pinstripes. He was an NL All Star
three-times as a Phillie (once with CA Angels). He won seven Gold Gloves
and was a member of the Phillies 1980 World Series Championship.
Boone joined the Phillies Wall of Fame in 2005.

Dave Schultz – Flyers/LW (1973-76) Dave "the Hammer" Schultz was one
of the most feared enforcers in the NHL. He was an integral part of the
intimidation factor of the Broad Street Bullies. His 472 PIMs in 1974-75 is

still an NHL Record. Schultz sits at #35 on the NHL's all-time career PIM's leaders and is the only player in the top 50 to play less than 11 seasons (9). His career average of 4.29 PIMs per game ranks 4th all-time in the NHL among players with at least 2000 PIM's (Shane Churla 4.71, Chris Nilan 4.42, Kelly Chase 4.40).   Schultz was more than a goon that could throw them, however, scoring 20 goals for the Flyers on their way to their first Stanley Cup. "The Hammer" was inducted into the Flyers Hall of Fame in 2009.

Aaron McKie – Sixers/G-F (1997-05 as player, 2007-13 as assistant coach) Aaron McKie was born and raised in Philly. He attended Simon Gratz HS and Temple University. He was a 1st round draft pick (17th overall) in the 1994 NBA Draft selected by the Portland Trail Blazers. He was a Sixer standout in 2001 helping the Sixers to the NBA Finals, and winning the NBA's Sixth Man Award.

Juan Samuel – Phillies/OF-INF (1983-89 as player, 2011-17 as coach) Juan Samuel was a slick-hitting speedy OF/INF throughout the 1980's. He was a member of the Phillies 1983 World Series team that lost to the Baltimore Orioles. Sammy was twice an All Star for the Phillies and won a Silver Slugger in 1987. Sammy was the Sporting News Rookie of the Year in 1984 when he led league in triples (19), ABs (701), was 2nd in SBs (72), 3rd in doubles (36), total bases (310), and extra base hits (70), and 4th in hits (191), and runs scored (105). Samuel was the 1st MLB player ever to have 10+ doubles, triples, homers, and stolen bases in each of his first four seasons. He was one triple short of making it five years in a row. The speedy Samuel finished his Phillies career with 249 stolen bases, good for 8th all-time. Samuel entered the Phillies Walk of Fame in 2008.

Did you know...

... In 1975, capitalizing on his unprecedented popularity in Philadelphia as "the Hammer", Flyers enforcer Dave Schultz released a 45 rpm record of the kitschy "Penalty Box."

Did you know... During the 2008 season, the Eagles had two special-teams rookie standouts. Rookie DeSean Jackson handled the punt returns and Quintin Demps handled kick-offs. Jackson broke the Eagles rookie records with 50 punt returns and 440 punt return yards. Demps broke the rookie record with 52 kick-off returns, and 1.314 return yards.

... Phillies catcher Bob Boone is a descendant of American Pioneer Daniel Boone.

... Flyers tough guy Dave Schultz scored two hat tricks during his Flyers career. He scored them one week apart during the 1973-74 season. His 1st was against the New York Rangers on January 3rd, 1974. One week later, on January 10th, 1974, he scored his second hat trick vs Minnesota North Stars.

... Phillies Juan Samuel's 701 ABs in 1984 set an NL record for right-handed hitters.

Even up...

8... Flyers goalie Pelle Lindbergh played 8 games in both his first and his last season (1981-82 and 1985-86).

8... NHL Record points in a game for a defenseman. On December 11th, 1977, Flyers defenseman Tom Bladon scored an NHL-record 8 points (4 goals and 4 assists). Hall of Famer and one-time Flyer Paul Coffey later tied the record while with Edmonton. Bladon was also an NHL record +10 that night.

9

Nick Foles – Eagles/QB (2012-14, 2017-present) On November 3rd, 2013 in a 49-20 win over the Oakland Raiders, Foles catapulted himself into the record books with a stellar 7 TD performance. Of the 8 QB's who have thrown for 7 TD's in a game, Foles is the only player in NFL history to do so with a perfect passer rating of 158.3. He had more TD's than incompletions in that game. Foles threw 19 TD's in 2013 before throwing his 1st interception. It's the 2nd longest streak in NFL history. On the season, Foles was an insane 27 TD's to 2 INTs, the highest TD-INT ratio in NFL history. His season passer rating of 119.0 is the league's 3rd highest ever. Foles was the Pro Bowl MVP in 2014. Foles returned to the Eagles in 2017 to back-up Carson Wentz. Foles became the starter in week 14 when Wentz went down with a season-ending knee injury. Foles led the Eagles to Super Bowl LII with playoff wins over the Atlanta Falcons and Minnesota Vikings. In Super Bowl LII, Foles became the NFL's first player to both throw and catch a TD pass in the Super Bowl after catching a TD pass from Trey Burton. Foles was named MVP of Super Bowl LII leading the Eagles to their first Super Bowl championship in franchise history.

Von Hayes – Phillies/OF-1B (1983-91) Von Hayes was a smooth hitting OF/1B known more for how he got to Phillies, than what he did for the Phillies. On December 9th, 1982, Hayes was traded to the Phillies from the Cleveland Indians for Julio Franco, Manny Trillo, Jay Baller, George Vukovich, and Jerry Willard. He quickly became known as "5 for 1".

While it was nearly impossible to live up to the hype of being traded for five players, Hayes did enjoy some success with the Phillies. Hayes was the first player in MLB history to hit 2 HRs in the 1st inning of a game, doing so on 6/11/1985. He smacked a lead-off dinger off Mets starter Tom Gorman, and later that inning he knocked a grand slam off reliever Calvin Schiraldi. The Phils won the game 26-7. Hayes led the NL in Runs and Doubles in 1986. The 1989 NL All Star was nicknamed "purple" by ESPN's Chris Berman, calling him Von "Purple" Hayes.

Andre Iguodala – Sixers/F-G (2004-12) The Sixers selected Iguodala 9th overall in the 2004 NBA Draft. He was named to the 2004-05 NBA All-Rookie team. Iggy was an NBA All-Star in his last season as a Sixer in 2011-12. Iguodala was a very durable player in his time as a Sixer. He didn't miss a single game in his first four seasons and only missed six games in his first six seasons. Iggy was the NBA Finals MVP 2014-15 for the Golden State Warriors.

Ivan Provorov – Flyers/D (2016-present) Ivan Provorov is a smooth-skating, intelligent defenseman selected by the Flyers 7th overall in the 2015 NHL Entry Draft. Provorov had an exceptional rookie season winning the Barry Ashbee Award as the Flyers most-outstanding defenseman. Provy was only the 3rd D-Man in team history to win the award as a rookie (Norm Barnes, Shayne Gostisbehere). On Dec 3rd, 2016 vs Chicago Black Hawks, Provy became the 1st Flyer D-man in team history to beat a goalie twice in under a minute when he scored the game-tying goal against Chicago goalie Scott Darling and 33 seconds later scored the game-winner.

Bob Kelly – Flyers/RW-LW (1971-80) Bob "the Hound" Kelly was a significant part of the Broad Street Bullies toughness. Kelly was not only one of the league's most-feared enforcers, he, like teammate Dave Schultz, could also put the puck in the net. In his ten seasons in the orange and black, Kelly scored 14 or more goals five times and potted 22 in 1976-77. Kelly's greatest moment was scoring the Stanley Cup-winning goal for the Flyers on May 27th, 1975 against the Buffalo Sabres in Buffalo. Kelly flew down the ice like a runaway train, and followed the puck around behind the net. The 5'10" Kelly out-hustled and out-muscled the 6'3" Sabre D-man Jerry "King Kong" Korab, came from behind the net and slid the puck past Sabre goalie Gerry Desjardins 11 seconds into the 3rd period of game 6. The Flyers won the game 2-0 to win their 2nd Stanley Cup.

Sonny Jurgensen – Eagles/QB (1957-63) Sonny Jurgensen won his only NFL Championship in 1960 as the Eagles back-up QB. Jurgensen was selected for the NFL's All-Decade team for the 1960's. He is also a member of the Eagles Hall of Fame and the Washington Redskins Ring of Fame. Jurgensen is in the Football Hall of Fame. Christian "Sonny" Jurgensen's middle name is Adolph.

Did you know...

... Ollie Matson (Eagles 1964-66) was once traded for 9 players in 1959. In 1952 at the Summer Olympics in Helsinki, Finland, he medaled twice for team USA in track, winning the bronze in the men's 400m, and a silver medal in the Men's 4x400m relay.

... Eagles QB Nick Foles tied an NFL record with his 25th consecutive completion (Golden Tate 7 yards) in a single game on December 30th, 2018 in a 24-0 win over the Washington Redskins. (Ryan Tannehill, Philip Rivers).

... Eagles QB Nick Foles had a franchise-record 471 passing yards in a 32-30 come from behind win over the Houston Texans on October 23rd, 2018.

... On February 8th, 2018, Flyers defenseman Ivan Provorov scored a 200-foot empty net goal vs Montreal Canadiens.

... On April 11th, 2018, in a playoff game vs Pittsburgh Penguins, Flyers defenseman Ivan Provorov took a shot from the top of the face-off circle that hit Penguins defenseman Kris Letang in the skate, and broke the puck in half.

Oddly enough...

9... of the top 35 all-time NBA Blocks Leaders played for the Sixers; Caldwell Jones 35th, Samuel Dalembert 33rd, Benoit Benjamin 32nd, Moses Malone 26th, Elton Brand 22nd, Theo Ratliff 19th, Manute Bol 15th, Shawn Bradley 14th, and Dikembe Mutombo 2nd.

9... Sixers Dana Barros set a team record with 9 three-pointers in a 108-107 loss to the Phoenix Suns on January 27th, 1995.

9... Different Flyer goalies have hit the 30+ wins mark in a season. Three of them did it back to back to back (Lindbergh 1985, Froese 1986, Hextall 1987).

10

Maurice Cheeks – Sixers/G (1978-89 as a player, 1994-01 as assistant coach, 2005-08 as Head Coach) Maurice Cheeks was a standout defensive player for the Sixers and was a key performer in their 1983 NBA Championship. Mo was a four-time NBA All Star, and was named to the NBA All Defensive 1st team four times, and 2nd team once. Cheeks is the Sixers all-time leader in assists with 6,212 and steals with 1,942. Cheeks is one of only three former Sixers players to have also been an assistant coach and head coach for the team (Matt Goukas, Fred Carter) Cheeks is 5th in the NBA all-time in steals, and 13th all-time in assists. The Sixers retired Mo's #10 in 1995.

Darren Daulton – Phillies/C (1983-97) Darren "Dutch" Daulton made his MLB debut with the Phillies in 1983, but became their full-time starter in 1988. On August, 15th, 1990, Dutch caught Terry Mulholland's No-Hitter, a 6-0 home win over the San Francisco Giants. Daulton had his best years in 1992 and 1993, leading the league in RBI's and winning the Silver Slugger Award in '92 and as the leader of Macho Row, going to the World Series in 1993. Daulton finished 6th, and 7th respectively in NL MVP voting. The three-time NL All Star won both a World Series with the Florida Marlins in 1997, and NL Comeback Player of the Year as voted by his peers. Dutch was ranked as the 25th best catcher of all time in the 2001 edition of Historical Baseball Abstract. In 2007, Daulton published the book, "If They Only Knew", about the paranormal and occultism. Dutch was added to the Phillies Wall of Fame in 2010. He succumbed to brain cancer in 2017.

Larry Bowa – Phillies/SS (1970-81 player, 2001-04 manager, 1989-96 and 2014-17 coach) Larry Bowa was a phenomenal defensive shortstop for the Phillies and a firebrand on the diamond. Bowa was 3rd in Rookie of the Year voting in 1970, won two Gold Gloves (1972, 78), and was 3rd in NL MVP voting in 1978. Bowa, a career .260 hitter batted .305 in 1975. The five-time NL All-Star was an important piece in the Phillies 1st World Series Championship in 1980. Bowa hung up his glove in 1981 with the NL record for games at shortstop (2222), single season fielding pct. (.991 in 1979), and had led the league in fielding pct. a record six times. His Career fielding pct. of .980 was also the NL's best at the time (these records have since been eclipsed). Bowa was named 2001 NL Manager of the Year in his first year as a Phillies Manager. 2018 will be Bowa's 34th year in the Phillies organization. The Phillies added Bowa to the Wall of Fame in 1991.

John LeClair – Flyers/LW (1995-04)   Big "Johnny Vermont" was a high-scoring winger on the Flyers famed Legion of Doom line. LeClair had three consecutive 50-goal seasons (51 in 1995-96, 50 in 1996-97, and 51 in 1997-98). He was the first American-born NHL player to accomplish this. LeClair was awarded the Pelle Lindbergh Memorial Trophy in 1995, the Bobby Clarke Trophy in 1997, 1998, and the NHL Plus/Minus Award in 1997, 1999. The 5-time NHL All Star was inducted into the US Hockey Hall of Fame in 2009.

DeSean Jackson – Eagles/WR-PR (2008-13) DeSean Jackson was a 2008 2nd round pick for the Eagles. He burst on the scene with his blazing speed and penchant for dramatics. Jackson was the first player to be selected to the NFL Pro Bowl at two different positions when he was selected as both Wide Receiver and Kick Returner for the 2010 Pro Bowl. On December 19th, 2010, DeSean Jackson capped off a miraculous comeback win over the New York Giants, known as the "Miracle of the Meadowlands II." Jackson returned a Matt Dodge punt 65 yards for the TD as time expired. The Eagles scored 28 points in the final seven and a half minutes. Jackson became the first player in NFL history to return a game-winning TD punt as time expired.   In 2013, NFL.com readers voted Jackson's TD return the greatest play of all time (over 58 million votes).

Did you know...

... Flyers Bill Clement (current Flyers broadcast team) had the 1st penalty shot in team history on March 7th, 1974 vs. Detroit Red Wings. Clement did not score.

Even up...

10... Tom Bladon's 4 goal 4 assist night on 12/11/77 netted him a +10 for the evening. It's the highest single game plus/minus in NHL history.

10 – Phillies slugger Ryan Howard had a Home Run every 10 At Bats during the 2006 season, a team record.

11

Jimmy Rollins – Phillies/SS (2000-14) Jimmy "J-Roll" Rollins was the greatest shortstop to ever wear a Phillies uniform. The four-time Gold Glove winner (2007-09, 2012) was dynamic on the diamond, and dynamic at the plate. J-Roll is the team's all-time leader in ABs (8,628), Hits (2,306), and 2Bs (479). Rollins is second all-time on the Phillies list for games played (2,090), stolen bases (453), and total bases (3,655). J-Roll is also third in runs scored (1,325), and triples (111), sixth in walks (753), eighth in runs batted in (887), and ninth in HRs (216). Rollins won a World Series with the Phillies in 2008, was NL MVP, and Silver Slugger Award winner in 2007, Roberto Clemente Award winner in 2014, and only one of four Major leaguers ever in the 20-20-20-20 Club (38 doubles, 20 triples, 30 HRs, 41 SBs in 2007). The three-time NL All-Star was third in Rookie-of-the-Year voting in 2001, had a 38-game hitting streak in 2005-06, and led the NL in stolen bases (46) in 2001.

Norm Van Brocklin – Eagles/QB (1958-60) Norm "the Dutchman" Van Brocklin quarterbacked the Eagles to their 1960 NFL Championship. The Eagles defeated the Green Bay Packers 17-13, giving Vince Lombardi the only finals loss of his career. Van Brocklin was the NFL MVP during that 1960 championship season, the Bert Bell Award winner, and his third Pro Bowl as an Eagle. Van Brocklin entered the Pro Football Hall of Fame in 1971, and the Eagles Hall of Fame in 1987.

Carson Wentz – Eagles/QB (2016-Present) Carson Wentz was taken 2nd overall in the 2016 NFL Draft. Wentz was the first rookie QB in 46 years win his first two NFL games while throwing zero interceptions. His 379 completions by a rookie QB in 2016 is an NFL record. The 379 completions is also a team record, as is his 607 pass attempts. In week 14 of the 2017 season, Wentz threw an Eagles team record 33rd TD pass of the season (vs Los Angeles Rams 12/10/17) before leaving the game with a season-ending knee injury. In his short career thus far, Wentz is two-time NFC Offensive Player-of-the-Week (wk #3 2016, wk#7 2017), and was the NFC Offensive Player-of-the-Month (October 2017). Wentz watched from the sidelines as his Eagles defeated the New England Patriots in Super Bowl LII for the team's first ever Super Bowl Championship.

Caldwell Jones – Sixers/C (1976-82) Caldwell Jones was selected 14th overall by the Sixers in the 1973 NBA Draft. A defensive stalwart, Jones finished his pro career with 10,068 points in 1,227 games. He is the only player in NBA history to achieve the 10,000 point milestone, and take over 1,200 games to do it. Jones was a two-time NBA All-Defensive First Team (1981, 82). He is 35th on NBA career Blocks list (1,517). On 9/15/82, the Sixers traded Caldwell Jones and a #1 pick (Rodney McRae) to the Houston Rockets for Moses Malone.

Travis Konecny – Flyers/RW (2016 - Present) Travis Konecny was selected 24th overall by the Flyers in the 2015 NHL Entry Draft. He made the team as a 19-yr old in 2016. Konecny solidified himself as a top six forward spending significant time on the Flyers top line in 2018. He finished the season with career-highs in Goals, Assists, Points, plus/minus. Konecny was the NHL's 2015 E.J. McGuire Award of Excellence winner.

Jrue Holiday – Sixers/PG (2009-13) Jrue Holiday was drafted by the Sixers 17th overall in the 2009 NBA Draft. The 2013 NBA All-Star was the youngest All-Star in franchise history. Jrue played 9 games with his older brother Justin at the end of the Sixers' 2012-13 season.

Did you know...

... Flyer winger Ron Flockhart scored the fastest two goals by one player in team history when he scored two goals 8 seconds apart in an 8-2 win over the St. Louis Blues on December 6th, 1981.

... Sixers Sudanese-born Manute Bol claims to have killed a lion with a spear growing up in a Dinka village in Africa.

... On July 4th, 1976, our nation's bicentennial, Phillies catcher Tim McCarver hit a grand slam home run but passed the runner at 1st base and was called out.

... During the 1992-93 season, the Flyers had their only father-son combo. Bill Dineen was the team's Head Coach, and his son Kevin Dineen was 4th on the team in scoring. It's also the only season in Flyers history where the team had no captain. The following season Terry Simpson took over as Head Coach, and Kevin Dineen was named the team's 10th captain.

Did you know...

... Flyers forward Travis Konecny is second cousins with Vancouver Canucks forward Bo Horvat.

... On September 27th, 2009, Phillies shortstop Jimmy Rollins hit his 21st homer of the season off Milwaukee Brewers pitcher Dave Bush, in a 6-5 Phillies win. The lead-off homer was the 217th home run of the season for the Phillies, breaking their 2006 team-record of 216. Second baseman Miguel Cairo hit a 4th inning homer on the last day of the season, a 7-6 win over the Florida Marlins (10/4/2009) giving the Phillies their current team-record of 224 home runs in a season. It was the only HR Miguel Cairo ever hit for the Phils.

... The Sixers have had two of the three tallest NBA players ever. 7'7" Manute Bol (1990-94) and 7'6" Shawn Bradley (1993-95). The two towers played together for 4 games in 1994. 7'7" Gheorghe Muresan (1993-2000) a former Washington Bullet and New Jersey Net, was the other tallest.

... Eagles KR Josh Huff had a team-record 107-yard kickoff return for a TD on November 23rd, 2014 vs Tennessee Titans.

Oddly enough...

11... HOF Flyers goalie Bernie Parent scored 11 points (all assists) during his Flyers career, good for 2nd best in team history (Ron Hextall – 28).

12

Randall Cunningham – Eagles/QB (1985-95) The Ultimate Weapon is widely considered one of the top five Quarterbacks in Eagles history. Cunningham was a mix of athleticism and speed. He was one of the best scrambling quarterbacks in history. While doubling as a punter, Cunningham smashed a 91-yard punt against the New York Giants on 12/3/89. Cunningham was a four-time Pro Bowler, winning the Pro Bowl MVP in 1989. His 106.0 passer rating in 1998 led the league. His career rushing average of 6.62 yards per carry is still an Eagles team record. Cunningham was a three-time Bert Bell Award winner, 1990 NFC Player of the Year, 1992 NFL Comeback Player of the Year, and was inducted into the Eagles Hall of Fame in 2009.

Simon Gagne – Flyers/LW (1999-13) Simon Gagne was a smooth-skating fan favorite for the orange and black. The two-time NHL All-Star was named to the NHL All-Rookie team in 1999, awarded the Pelle Lindbergh Memorial Trophy in 2001, the Bob Clarke Trophy in 2006 and 2007 and the Toyota Cup for 2001-02, 2005-06, and 2006-07. Simon netted 47 goals for the Flyers in 2005-06. Gagne won a gold medal with Team Canada at the Salt Lake 2002 Winter Olympics and went on to win a Stanley Cup in 2012 with the Los Angeles Kings.

Tim Kerr – Flyers/RW (1981-91) Tim Kerr was a dominant power forward for the Flyers in the mid 1980's. His four straight 50-goal seasons (54, 54, 58, 58) is still a team record. The three-time NHL All Star was an undrafted free agent signed by the Flyers in 1980. His 34 Power Play Goals in 1985-86 is still an NHL record. Kerr won the Bill Masterton Trophy in 1988-89. Kerr is 2nd all-time in career playoff shooting pct. (20.3). Kerr scored the fastest 4 goals in one period in a playoff game (8:16) 4/13/85 at New York Rangers.

Did you know...

... Flyers great Tim Kerr scored 4 goals in a game 5 times, the most in team history.

... Flyers Simon Gagne was born on February 29th, 1980 on leap day. Gagne will celebrate his 10th birthday in 2020.

... On March 6th, 1971, Flyers winger Gary Dornhoefer notched the team's 1st-ever natural hat trick.

... Phillies 2009 NLCS game 4 hero Matt Stairs hit the last home run called by Phillies legendary play-by-play announcer Harry Kalas. Stairs hit a game-winning pinch-hit homer in the top of the 9th on April 12th, 2009 in a Phillies 7-5 win over the Colorado Rockies. Harry Kalas passed away the next day.

Did you know...

... On April 8th, 2017 the Phillies scored a team-record 12 1st inning runs vs Washington Nationals at Citizens Bank Park. The Phillies had zero homers in the inning but they did have a triple, three doubles, and nine total hits to go along with 4 walks.

... On September 20th, 1992, in a 3-2 loss to the Pittsburgh Pirates, Phillies 2B Mickey Morandini had an unassisted triple play in the 6th inning. He caught a Jeff King line drive, stepped on second base and then tagged the runner coming from 1st. It was just the 9th unassisted triple play of the modern era.

Even up...

12... The Flyers have had 12 players whose last name began with Z (Zarley Zalapski, Larry Zeidel, Valeri Zelepukin, Jason Zent, Rob Zepp, Rob Zettler, Peter Zezel, Alexei Zhamnov, Nikolai Zherdev, Alexei Zhitnik, Harry Zolnierczyk, and Dainius Zubrus.

12... Eagles QB Donovan McNabb was sacked an NFL-record 12 times in a 16-3 loss to New York Giants on September 30th, 2007.

12... Gerald Henderson and Gerald Henderson jr are the only father-son connection in Sixers team history. Like father, like son, they both had a Player Efficiency Rating of 13.4, and both wore #12 as Sixers.

13

Wilt Chamberlain/C – (Philadelphia Warriors – 1959-65), Sixers (1965-68).   Wilt the Stilt Chamberlain was one of the most dominating basketball players of all time. His list of NBA records is as long as his 7'1" frame. The four-time NBA MVP (1-Warriors, 3-Sixers) was the 1960 NBA All-Star game MVP (Warriors) and Rookie of the Year. Chamberlain was an NBA All-Star five times with the Warriors, and four times with the Sixers. He was the NBA scoring champ seven times (1960-68), four-time Rebounding Champ as a Warrior, and three times as a Sixer, and led the NBA in assists in 1968 (Sixers). Chamberlain holds the team record for points in a game with the Warriors (100 vs. New York Knicks 3/2/62) and the Sixers (68 vs Chicago Bulls 12/16/67). In his rookie season 1961-62, Chamberlain missed only seven minutes of playing time the entire season! His 48.5 minutes per game average is an NBA record that is unlikely to ever be broken. Chamberlain owns the highest single season scoring average (50.4 points per game) and had a team record 43 rebounds in one game (3/6/65). He has the only double-triple-double in NBA history scoring 22 points, with 25 rebounds and 21 assists vs. Detroit Pistons on 2/2/68.

Just how dominant was Chamberlain? No other NBA player has ever averaged 30 points per game and 20 rebounds per game over an entire NBA season. The Big Dipper not only managed that feat seven times, but averaged those numbers for his entire CAREER! The Warriors, Sixers, and Lakers all retired Wilt's #13. He was selected for the NBA 35th and

50th Anniversary teams, and was inducted into the Naismith Memorial Basketball Hall of Fame in 1978. Chamberlain still holds over 70 NBA records... THAT'S how dominant he was!

Did you know...

... The Flyers have scored 13 goals in a game twice in their history. They were both during the calendar year of 1984. They defeated the Pittsburgh Penguins 13-4 on March 22nd, 1984 and defeated the Vancouver Canucks 13-2 on October 18th, 1984.

... Wilt Chamberlain played for the Harlem Globetrotters prior to the start of his Hall of Fame NBA career.

Oddly enough...

13... Lucky Friday the 13th for Flyers Center Sean "Jason Voorhees" Couturier. On Friday April 13th, 2012 in a playoff game in Pittsburgh, Coots had a hat trick and an assist. Exactly 6 years later, on Friday April 13th, 2018 in a playoff game in Pittsburgh, Coots had 3 assists giving him 7 career playoff points, all coming on Friday the 13ths in Pittsburgh.

13... Eagles WR Nelson Agholor is the 9th player in team history to wear the #13.

14

Pete Rose – Phillies/1B (1979-83) Charlie Hustle was the greatest hitter in MLB history. His 4,256 hits, 3,215 singles, 3,462 games and 14,053 at bats are still major league records. The Phillies acquired Rose in 1979 with the hope he was the missing piece to put them over the top to win a World Series. The Phillies accomplished that goal in 1980, and returned to the finals in 1983. Rose was a four-time All Star as a Phillie, and won the Silver Slugger Award in 1981. Over his long and illustrious playing career, Pete Rose was an All Star seventeen times, at five different positions. Rose's off-the-field issues and lifetime ban are well-documented, but his on-the-field prowess made Rose one of the game's all-time legends.

Jim Bunning – Phillies/P (1964-67, 1970-71) As a Phillie, Jim Bunning led the National League in strikeouts in 1967, and made the NL All Star team in 1964 and 1966. On Father's Day, June 21st, 1964, during the first game of a double header against the New York Mets at Shea Stadium, Bunning threw the 7th Perfect Game in MLB History. Bunning's perfect game was the first regular season perfect game in the National League since 1880! It was also the first no-hitter thrown by a Phillie hurler in 58 years. Jim Bunning threw a no-hitter, reached 100 wins, and notched 1000 KO's in both the American League and National League. Bunning was the first pitcher in the game's history to accomplish this. Bunning entered the Phillies Wall of Fame in 1984, was inducted into the Baseball Hall of Fame in 1996, and the Phillies retired Bunning's #14 in 2001. Jim Bunning served as US Senator from Kentucky 1999-2011. He is the only member of the Baseball Hall of Fame to also serve in the US Senate.

Henry Bibby – Sixers/PG (1976-80) (assistant coach 2006-08) Henry Bibby spent 4 seasons with the Sixers missing only one game during his Sixers career. During his time with the team, the Sixers went to two NBA Finals (1977, 80), losing both. He averaged nearly 30 minutes per game with 4.6 assists and 10.1 points. Henry was an assistant coach under Maurice Cheeks.

Sean Couturier – Flyers/C (2011-present) Sean Couturier was selected by the Flyers 8th overall in the 2011 NHL Entry Draft. Couturier made his reputation as an outstanding defensive forward over his first six seasons. He was teamed with Flyers Captain Claude Giroux for the 2017-18 season and enjoyed career highs in Goals (31), Assists (45), Points (76), and Plus/Minus (+34). On March 20th, 2018, Couturier scored his 100th NHL goal vs Detroit Red Wings on the power play. The tally also gave him his 1st 30-goal season. Couturier won the Pele Lindbergh Award, the Yanick Dupre Class Guy Award, and the Gene Hart Memorial Award for the 2017-18 season, and finished 2nd in voting for the NHL's Frank J Selke Trophy.

Joe Watson – Flyers/D (1967-68 to 1977-78) Joe Watson was a member of the Flyers Broad Street Bullies teams that won back to back Stanley Cups in 1974, and '75. Watson was the 2nd skater selected by the Flyers in the 1967 NHL Expansion Draft. Joe and his younger brother Jim were the 2nd of 5 brother combos to play for the Flyers spending 5 years together in the orange and black (1973-78). Watson, not known as a goal-scoring defenseman, scored just 38 goals in 11 seasons for the Flyers. However, during the famous 1976 game against the vaunted Soviet team, Watson scored a short-handed goal against legendary Russian netminder Vladislav Tretiak. Flyers coach Fred Shero commented afterwards that Watson's goal "set Russian hockey back 25 years."

Did you know...

... Phillies great Jim Bunning's perfect game on June 21st, 1964 was game 1 of a double header against the NY Mets. Rick Wise won game 2 of the twinbill for the Phillies in his MLB debut.

... Sixer Henry Bibby's son Mike Bibby played 14 years in the NBA. Bibby's brother, Jim Bibby, was a 12-year Major League baseball pitcher.

... Flyers Sean Couturier led the NHL in Total Goals on Ice For, with 142 in 2018.

... Flyers Sean Couturier's father Sylvain Couturier played parts of three NHL seasons with the Los Angeles Kings.

... Flyers Sean Couturier's hometown of Bathurst, New Brunswick named the street leading to the town ice rink where Coots played in his youth, "Sean Couturier Way."

Even up...

14... The Phillies have made the postseason just 14 times in their 136-year history. They also lost 100+ games in a season 14 times.

14... Flyers Ville Leino holds the NHL record for playoff assists in a playoff season by a rookie with 14 assists during the 2009-2010 NHL Playoffs.

15

Steve Van Buren – Eagles/HB (1944-51) Steve Van Buren was one of the greatest players to ever wear an Eagle uniform. Wham Bam Van Buren played his entire eight-year career with the Eagles. He was the 5th overall selection in the 1944 NFL Draft. The six-time 1st-team All Pro led the league in yards rushing four times, and rushing TD's four times. Van Buren was a huge part of the Eagles back-to-back NFL Championships in 1948, '49. Van Buren scored the only TD in their first championship, and rushed for 196 yards in their second. Van Buren remains the Eagles career rushing TD leader (78). He was named to the NFL 1940's All-Decade team, and the NFL 75th Anniversary All-Time Team. The Eagles retired Van Buren's #15 and entered him into their Hall of Fame. Van Buren was inducted into the Pro Football Hall of Fame in 1965.

Hal Greer – Sixers/Nationals/G (1958-73) Hal Greer was a mainstay on the Sixers backcourt for 15 seasons (five w/ Syracuse Nationals). Greer is the franchise's all-time leader in games played (1,122), Minutes played (39,788), FG's (8,504), and points (21,586). The Ten-time NBA All Star was the All Star MVP in 1968. Greer won an NBA Championship as a member of the Sixers in 1967. He was selected as part of the NBA's 50th Anniversary All-Time Team. Greer is in the Sixers Hall of Fame and had his #15 retired. He was inducted into the Pro Basketball Hall of Fame in 1982.

Dick Allen – Phillies/1B-OF (1963-69, 1975-76) Dick Allen was a premiere slugger during his MLB career. During his time with the Philies, Allen was Rookie-of-the-Year in 1964, and was a three-time NL All Star (1965-67). His sensational Rookie season saw Allen lead the league in runs (125), triples (13) and finish 5th in batting average (.318). He also finished 3rd in Slugging Pct. (.557), 3rd in hits (201), 4th in doubles (38), 7th in HR's (29), and 1st in total bases (352). Dick Allen was enshrined on the Phillies Wall of Fame in 1994.

Did you know...

... On April 12th, 1968, Flyers Andre Lacroix scored the 1st power play goal in team history in a 5-2 loss to St. Louis Blues.

... Eagles Hall of Famer Steve Van Buren was born in La Ceiba, Hondurus on December 28th, 1920.

Oddly enough...

15... NHL record for consecutive games scoring by a rookie defenseman – Flyers Shayne Gostisbehere January 19th, 2016 to February 20th, 2016.

16

Bob Clarke – Flyers/C (player 1969-84) (GM 1984-90, 1994-06), (executive 2007-present) Robert Earle Clarke was one of the greatest team captains in the history of the game. Clarkie played his entire 15-year career in the orange and black and captained the team to two Stanley Cup Championships. Clarke served as captain from 1973-79 and 1982-84. Clarke has served as team captain, assistant coach, General Manager, and Senior Vice President. He has been to four Stanley Cup finals as a player, three finals as a GM, and one finals as Sr.VP.

As a player, Clarkie was fierce and courageous. On March 19th, 1981, Clarke was hit in the face with a shot off the stick of linemate Reg Leach. Clarkie got stitched up and returned to score his 19th goal of the season. It was his 1,000th NHL point.

Clarkie was a three-time Hart Trophy winner, an eight-time NHL All Star, a Frank J Selke Trophy winner (1983), and a Bill Masterton Trophy winner (1972). He had three 100+ point seasons, and is the Flyers all-time leader in games played (1,144), assists (852), points (1,210), and shorthanded goals (32). The Bobby Clarke Trophy is awarded annually to the Flyers team MVP. In junior hockey, the WHL gives the Bobby Clarke Trophy to the league's leading scorer.

In 1998, the Hockey News ranked Clarke 24th on their Top NHL Players of All-Time list. Clarke's #16 has been retired by the team and he is a member of the Flyers Hall of Fame. Clarke was inducted into the Hockey Hall of Fame in 1987.

Norm Snead – Eagles/QB (1964-70) Norm Snead was a Pro Bowl Quarterback who played 16 seasons in the NFL. The four-time Pro Bowler (once w/ Eagles '65) threw for over 30,000 yards in his career. Norm Snead is the last NFL quarterback to win a game with a passer rating of 0.0

Did you know…

… Flyers Hall of Famer Bobby Clarke wore the #36 sweater for two games during a road trip in 1981. His jersey had been stolen and the #36 was the only backup jersey available.

Even up…

16… The Flyers Legion of Doom line, with Eric Lindros, John LeClair, and Mikael Renberg totaled 16 points in a game against the Montreal Canadiens on February 6th, 1997. It was the most points in a single game for a Flyers line in team history. Three weeks later they did it again against the Ottawa Senators.

16… Eagles QB Carson Wentz threw a rookie-record 16 TD passes in 2016.

17

Harold Carmichael – Eagles/WR (1971-83) Harold Carmichael, at 6'8" was the tallest WR in NFL history. Carmichael was a four-time Pro Bowler (1973, 1978-80), and in 1973 led the NFL in receptions (67), receiving yards (1,116), receiving yards per game (79.7), and was 4th in receiving TDs (9). Carmichael holds the Eagles team career record for pass receptions (589), receiving yards (8,978), TDs (79), consecutive games played (162). In 1980 Carmichael made a catch in his 127th consecutive game, an NFL Record at the time. Carmichael has played the third-most games in team history. Carmichael was voted to the NFL 1970's All-Decade Team. He was inducted into the Eagles Hall of Fame in 1987

Rod Brind'Amour – Flyers/C (1991-2000) Rod the bod was a fan favorite with the Flyers and was well-known for his affinity for the weight room. During his time with the Flyers, Brind'Amour played an astounding 484 consecutive games. The 1992 NHL All Star played a total of 633 games for the orange and black. Brind'Amour finished his Flyers career 10th in goals (235) and 9th in points (601). Brind'Amour once scored two short-handed goals on the same power-play in the first round of the 1997 playoffs vs. Pittsburgh. Brind'Amour won the Bobby Clarke Trophy in 1992. He was traded to the Carolina Hurricanes along with Jean-Marc Pelletier in exchange for Keith Primeau. Brind'Amour went on to win two Frank J Selke Awards and a Stanley Cup with Carolina. Brind'Amour entered the Flyers Hall of Fame in 2015.

Scott Rolen – Phillies/3B (1996-02) Scott Rolen was a smooth-fielding, Gold Glove third baseman. In his first full MLB season, the Phillie rookie won NL Rookie-of-the-Year honors for 1997.   He was a seven-time NL All Star (once as a Phillie in 2002). Rolen was awarded four Gold Gloves during his time in Philly. Rolen's eight Gold Gloves are the third most of any third baseman in MLB history (Brooks Robinson-16, Mike Schmidt-10).

Wayne Simmonds – Flyers/RW (2011–Present) The Wayne Train has been a fan favorite since his arrival in Philly as part of the Mike Richards to the Los Angeles Kings deal. Simmonds is known for his scoring, his hustle, and his pugilistic exploits. The combination of which has earned Simmer three Gordie Howe hattricks (goal, assist, fight) to date. Oddly enough, Gordie Howe in his 26-year career only had two. Simmonds last goal of the 2014-15 season was his 100th as a Flyer.   Prior to the start of the 2018 season Simmonds had 163 goals and 39 fights for the orange and black. Simmonds was a first-time All Star in 2017 and led the way with three goals including the game-winner, earning the game's MVP.

Alshon Jeffery – Eagles/WR (2017-Present) Alshon Jeffery signed with the Eagles as a free agent for the 2017 season. Jeffery signed on for four more years during week 12 of the 2017 season.   Jeffery finished the regular season with 57 receptions for 789 yards and was 4th in the league in 2017 with 9 TD catches. Jeffery added 3 more TDs in the playoffs with 12 catches for 219 yards. Jeffery scored the Eagles' 1st TD on their way to winning Super Bowl LII.

Rhys Hoskins – Phillies/OF (2017-present) Rhys Hoskins made his MLB debut on August 10th, 2017. He started the month of August in AAA, and ended the month of August in the MLB record books. Hoskins hit 9 HRs in his first 16 games, 10 in his first 17, 11 in his first 18, and 12 in 24 games... all MLB records. He went on to be the fastest in MLB history for homers 9 thru 17. He tied Phillies record by hitting HRs in 5 consecutive games. He was also the first Phillie outfielder in 53 years to begin a triple play. One unbelievable start to a career. He finished 2017 with 18 HRs, 48 RBIs in 50 games and 170 ABs.

Did you know...

... Flyers winger Wayne Simmonds was once credited for scoring a goal that deflected off his forehead and into the net off a Brayden Schenn shot on March, 30th, 2012 vs. Ottawa Senators.

... Phillies Scott Rolen once scored on his own bunt vs Pittsburgh Pirates. He circled the bases but was not credited with a home run due to the two Pirate errors on the play.

Oddly enough...

17... Flyers winger Tim Kerr scored 17 hat tricks during his Flyers career, including 5 4-goal games. He also had 5 hat tricks during the 1984-85 season. All three feats are Flyers team records.

17... Flyers Shayne Gostisbehere holds the team record for goals by a rookie defenseman, scoring 17 during the 2015-16 season.

18

Mike Richards – Flyers/C (2005-11) Mike Richards was the 17th captain in Flyers team history. The two-time 30-goal scorer for the orange and black won the Gene Hart Memorial Trophy in 2008, the Bobby Clarke Trophy in 2008, 2009, the Toyota Cup in 2010, and in 2009 was runner-up for the NHL's Frank J Selke Trophy. Richards appeared in his only All Star game in 2008. Richards won the Calder Cup with the Philadelphia Phantoms in 2005, and won a Gold Medal at the 2010 Vancouver Olympics with Team Canada. Richards is the only NHL player with three shorthanded- goals while his team was two-men down. He's also the only player in NHL history to play in two playoff series where his team came back from 3-0 deficit to win the series (Flyers 2010 vs Boston Bruins, and Los Angeles Kings 2014 vs. San Jose Sharks).

Jeremy Maclin – Eagles/WR (2009-14) Jeremy Maclin was the Eagles first round selection in the 2009 NFL Draft. The fleet-footed receiver spent six seasons in Philadelphia, and was selected to the Pro Bowl in 2014, his last season as an Eagle. Though Maclin only played five seasons in Midnight Green (he sat out 2013 with torn ACL), he ranks 7th all-time in receiving TDs, 9th all-time in receptions, and 9th all-time in receiving yards. On January 9th, 2010 in Dallas, Maclin participated in his very first NFL playoff contest. Though the Eagles fell to the Dallas Cowboys 34-14 that day, Maclin became the youngest player in NFL history to score a postseason touchdown when he caught Michael Vick's 76-yard TD pass.

The pass was also Vick's longest TD pass of his career. Maclin finished the day with 146 yards receiving, breaking an Eagles postseason record that had stood for 22 years.

Ben Hawkins – Eagles/WR (1966-73) The Hawk, Ben Hawkins led the NFL in receiving yards in his second season with the birds. Hawkins played all but two of his games in Eagles Kelly Green, ending his career with two games for the Cleveland Browns in 1974. Hawkins played for the Philadelphia Bell in 1975. Hawkins is 10th all-time in Eagles' team history in receiving TDs, 10th all-time in receiving yards, and 19th all-time in receptions.

Did you know...

... Phillies 3B/1B Richie Hebner was a HS ice hockey standout and was offered a contract by the Boston Bruins before opting for Major League Baseball. Hebner's nickname was gravedigger. Hebner worked as a gravedigger during the off season early in his career.

... Flyers Mike Richards has had the most penalty shot attempts in team history. Richards was awarded 6 penalty shots during his stay in Philly (October 17th, 2006 vs Buffalo, November 21st, 2007 vs Carolina, April 15th, 2008 vs Washington, October 28th, 2008 vs Atlanta, March 20th, 2009 vs Buffalo, and January 23rd, 2010 vs Carolina. He only scored one of them (4/15/08 vs Wash).

... Flyers Hall of Famers Bobby Clarke and Eric Lindros each had a team-record 18-game point streak (Clarke – 1975, Lindros – 1999).

Even up...

18... Flyers goalie/GM Ron Hextall posted 18 shutouts during his Flyers career, 3rd-most in team history (Bernie Parent – 50, Roman Cechmanek - 20).

18... Flyers defensemen Doug Crossman (1987) and Chris Pronger (2010) hold the team record for points by a defenseman in a single playoff year with 18 points.

18... Sixers great Hal Greer had a team-record 18 FGs in one half in a 124-121 loss to the Chicago Bulls on Valentine's Day in 1959.

18... Sixers great Dolph Schayes went a perfect 18 for 18 in free throws three times during his Nationals/Sixers career. 1/10/57 vs Minneapolis, 3/9/57 vs Boston, and 10/24/60 vs LA Lakers.

18... On April 14th, 2018, the Sixers scored 18 3-point buckets in a 130-103 game 1 win over the Miami Heat in the 2018 playoffs. The Sixers shattered their previous team record of 11. They did it again in game 3, six days later.

19

Rick MacLeish – Flyers/C (1970-81, 1983-84) Slick skating Rick MacLeish was the first true "sniper" of the Flyers with his wicked wrister, and effortless skating. MacLeish was the Flyers first 50-goal scorer and second 100-point scorer, notching his 100th point (his 50th goal) just two days after Bobby Clarke hit the century mark at the end of the 1972-73 season. MacLeish scored 30 or more goals seven times for the Flyers. His biggest goal came on May 19th, 1974 in game six of the 1973-74 Stanley Cup Finals. MacLeish deflected a Moose Dupont shot past Boston Bruins goaltender Gilles Gilbert in the first period. It was the game's only goal as the Flyers won game 6, 1-0 and captured their first Stanley Cup. MacLeish, a three-time NHL All Star entered the Flyers Hall of Fame in 1990.

Greg Luzinski – Phillies/LF (1970-80) Greg "the Bull" Luzinski was a slugging left fielder for the Phillies throughout the 70's. The four-time NL All Star led the NL in RBIs in 1975 and was MVP runner-up in 1975 and 1977. Luzinski made his Major League debut at 19 yrs old. His last game as a Phillies was the 1980 World Series clincher against the Kansas City Royals. In the 1980 NLCS against the Houston Astros, Luzinski had two game-winning hits. Luzinski pounded 307 HRs and 1,128 RBIs in his career. He won the Roberto Clemente Award in 1978, and entered the Phillies Wall of Fame in 1998.

Mikael Renberg – Flyers/RW (1993-97, 1998-2000) Mikael Renberg was one-third of the legendary Legion of Doom (John LeClair, Eric Lindros). Renberg set a Flyers Rookie Record with 82 points (38g-44a) in 83 games during the 1993-94 season. Renberg never topped his rookie campaign but he did score 20 or more goals four times for the orange and black. Renberg was the very first recipient of the Pelle Lindbergh Memorial Award in 1994. He was also awarded the Yanick Dupre Trophy in 1995. Renberg was a two-time Olympian with the Swedish National Team in 1998 and 2002.

Manny Trillo – Phillies/2B (1979-82) Manny Trillo was a good-hitting second baseman with a great glove and great arm. In four seasons in Philly, Trillo appeared in two All Star games, won three Gold Gloves, and two Silver Slugger Awards. Trillo was the 1980 NLCS MVP en route to the Phillies World Series win. In 1981, Trillo fielded 479 chances in a row without an error (a record since broken), and his 89 consecutive error-free games fell two short of Joe Morgan's record 91.

Did you know...

... Eagles kicker Tom Dempsey kicked a team-record 6 FGs on November 12th, 1972 vs. Houston Oilers.

Oddly enough...

19... Flyers sniper Reggie Leach scored an NHL record 19 goals in the 1976 NHL Playoffs (Edmonton's Jari Kurri tied the record in 1985 against the Flyers in the Cup-deciding game 5). Leach had scored 61 regular season goals, giving him a phenomenal 80 goals on the year.

19... Dave Hakstol became the 19th Head Coach in Flyers team history when he was hired prior to the 2015-16 NHL season.

20

Mike Schmidt – Phillies/3B (1972-1989) Michael Jack Schmidt was the greatest third baseman of all time. He played his entire stellar career with the Phillies and is the team's all-time leader in well over a dozen statistical categories. No other player in MLB history who played their entire career with one team hit as many home runs as Schmidt (548). Schmidt was a 12-time All Star, 10-time Gold Glover, 6-time Silver Slugger, 3-time league MVP, 8-time HR leader, 4-time RBI leader and was the World Series MVP in 1980. And who could ever forget the day Schmitty took the field in a long black wig and sunglasses! The Phillies retired Schmidt's #20 and added him to their wall of fame in 1990. He entered Cooperstown in 1995.

Brian Dawkins – Eagles/S (1996-2008) "Weapon X" was one of the greatest and most popular Eagles ever. B-Dawk was a 9-time Pro Bowler, 4-time 1st team All Pro, and 2-time 2nd team All Pro. Dawk is the only player in league history with 25 or more INTs (37), Forced Fumbles (36), and Sacks (26). His 36 Forced Fumbles were the most ever by an NFL Safety. Dawkins was the first NFL player to hit the 30-mark for INTs and Forced Fumbles, and is in the 20/20 Club with 26 Sacks and 37 INTs. Dawkins finished his career with 1,131 tackles. On September 29th, 2002, vs. the Houston Texans at Veterans Stadium, Dawkins recorded a sack, recovered a fumble, had an interception, and on a fake punt play had a 58-yard TD reception on a toss from Brian Mitchell. No other NFL player in the history of the game has accomplished this feat. Dawkins is second all-time on the Eagles games played list. Weapon X was selected to the NFL's 2000's All-Decade Team, the Eagles 75th Anniversary Team, and had his #20 retired by the Eagles in 2012. B-Dawk entered the Pro Football Hall of Fame in 2018.

Doug Collins – Sixers/G (1973-81 as a player, 2010-13 as coach) If you put a list together of the top dozen Sixers ever, Doug Collins is on your list. Collins was selected 1st overall by the Sixers in the NBA Draft on April 24th, 1973. Collins was selected to the NBA All Star team four years in a row. A devastating knee injury kept him from more. Collins was on the silver-medal winning US Men's basketball team at the 1972 Olympics. A controversial call allowed the Russians to win the gold medal. The US team did not accept their Silver medal in protest. Collins went on to coach the Sixers, finishing with a .478 winning percentage after three seasons. Illinois State University, where Collins was a first team All-American in 1973, honored Collins with a statue and the naming of the basketball court "Doug Collins Court at Redbird Arena.

Dave Poulin – Flyers/C (1983-90) Dave Poulin was an undrafted free-agent signing for the Flyers. While playing in Sweden, his coach Ted Sator, a Flyer scout at the time, sold the Flyers brass on Poulin's abilities. Poulin scored 20+ goals for the Flyers four times, and was the only Flyer to appear in the NHL's Rendezvous '87 series. Poulin is the only Flyer other than Bobby Clarke to win the Frank J Selke Award (1987). Poulin won the Yanick Dupre Award in 1984, captained the Flyers to two Stanley Cup Finals against the Edmonton Oilers (1985, 87) and won the

NHL's King Clancy Trophy in 1993. Poulin entered Flyers Hall of Fame in 2004.

Chris Pronger – Flyers/D (2009-11) Chris Pronger was a punishing NHL defenseman who spent his last two seasons with the Flyers. Pronger won the Barry Ashbee Trophy and Bobby Clarke Trophy in 2010 as the Flyers went to the Stanley Cup Finals. The following season he became the 18th captain in team history. A stick to the eye from Mikhail Grabovski in October of 2011 effectively ended Pronger's playing career. In 2015, Pronger was traded to the Phoenix Coyotes for salary cap reasons. Three days later Pronger was elected to the Hockey Hall of Fame. In his Hall of Fame career, Pronger was a six-time All Star, won the Norris Trophy, Hart Trophy, a Stanley Cup, and two Olympic gold medals with team Canada.

Andre Waters – Eagles/S (1984-93) Safety Andre "dirty" Waters was one of the fiercest hitters in the NFL. Waters' hit on LA Rams QB Jim Everett led to the Andre Waters Rule protecting quarterbacks in the pocket from being hit below the waist. Waters led the Eagles in tackles four times, had 15 career INTs, and scored a TD on a Reggie White sack and subsequent William Frizzell lateral in 1989. Dirty Waters was All NFC in 1991 as a part of Gang Green, one of the best defenses ever assembled. Waters was named to the Eagles 75th Anniversary team. Andre Waters struggled with depression after his playing career. His suicide and subsequent brain tissue examination and CTE diagnosis as featured in the 2015 movie Concussion helped change the protocols on head injuries in professional and amateur sports.

Eric Snow – Sixers/PG (1998-04) Eric Snow was an excellent defensive and passing point guard for the Sixers under Coach Larry Brown. Snow and Hall of Famer Allen Iverson formed a formidable backcourt tandem propelling the Sixers to the NBA Finals in 2001. Snow was All Defensive 2nd Team in 2003. He won the NBA Sportsmanship Award in 2000 and the J Walter Kennedy Citizenship Award in 2005. Snow played for three teams in his NBA career and went to the finals with all three... and lost all three.

Did you know...

... On April 17th, 1976 in a game against the Chicago Cubs, Mike Schmidt not only hit 4 Home Runs, but three of the four were off brothers. Schmidt hit his first two off starter Rick Reuschel, his 3rd off Mike Garman, and his 4th off Paul Reuschel. Schmidt finished with 8 RBIs. The game at Wrigley Field featured 9 home runs (6 by Phils) and was won by the Phillies 18-16 in 10 innings.

... Phillies great Mike Schmidt once hit the public address speaker in Houston's Astrodome. The speaker was 329 feet from Home plate and 117 feet above the playing surface. What could have been a 500+ foot Homer, only earned Schmidt a single.

... After the 1980 World Series, Phillies Mike Schmidt, Larry Bowa, Garry Maddox, Dick Ruthven, and Del Unser faced off against the Kansas City Royals' Dennis Leonard, Dan Quisenberry, Paul Splittorff, John Wathan, and Willie Wilson on the TV show Family Feud.

Did you know...

... Dave Poulin was the first Flyers captain in team history to not be drafted by the team (Entry Draft or Expansion Draft).

... Chris Pronger, on three occasions, led the team that traded for him to the Stanley Cup Finals.

... The Flyers all-time roster features players from 20 different nations.

... Phillies outfielder Roger Freed was the last Phillies player to wear #20 before Hall of Famer Mike Schmidt immortalized it.

... Brian Dawkins' only Super Bowl appearance was with the Eagles in 2004. The game was played in his hometown of Jacksonville, Florida.

Even up...

20... On April 7th, 2018, the Phillies defeated the Miami Marlins 20-1 at Citizens Bank Park. The Phillies trailed 1-0 before scoring 20 unanswered runs. Outfielder Aaron Altheer and third baseman Maikel Franco each hit a Grand Slam. The Phillies had scored 19 runs in their first 6 games of the season, total, before scoring 20 in their 7th game.

20... Phillies great Jimmy Rollins had a modern-era team-record 20 triples in 2007, the most for a Phillies player since 1897.

21

Eric Allen – Eagles/CB (1988-94) Eric Allen was an integral part of the Eagles Gang Green, one of the best defenses of all time. The six-time Pro Bowler, three-time All NFC and 1st Team All Pro had 7 career fumble recoveries, 54 INTs, and 8 TDs. Allen's 94-yard pick-six against the Jets in 1993 is quite possibly the greatest pick-six in NFL History. Allen is the only player in NFL history to twice have three pick-sixes in a season. His four pick-sixes in 1993 tied an NFL record. He was named to the NFL's 75th Anniversary team and entered the Eagles Hall of Fame in 2011.

Peter Forsberg – Flyers/C (2005-07)   Foppa was one of the greatest players of his generation. Forsberg was a Flyers 1st round draft pick in 1991. He was traded away as part of the deal that brought Eric Lindros to the Flyers. Though Forsberg would eventually wear the orange and black, he was near the end of his Hall of Fame career when that happened. Forsberg played less than two seasons in Philly but posted 115 pts in 100 games as a Flyer. He was also the 15th captain in team history taking over for retired Keith Primeau in 2006. Over his stellar career, Forsberg won a Calder Trophy, Art Ross Trophy, Hart Memorial Trophy, two Stanley Cups, the Yanick Dupre Award with the Flyers, and was named one of the 100 greatest players in NHL history. He entered the Hockey Hall of Fame in 2014.

Joel Embiid – Sixers/C (2014-present) Foot issues caused Embiid to sit out his first two seasons. Embiid was limited to 31 games during his third season and he was still named 1st Team All-Rookie. The Cameroonian showed in 2017-2018 that he was well worth the wait. Embiid was selected for his first NBA All Star game and led the Sixers back to the postseason. His season was cut short when he collided with teammate Markelle Fultz, breaking his orbital bone and requiring surgery. Embiid finished 3rd in voting for the NBA Defensive Player of the Year Award for 2017-18. The Process was also named 2nd team All-Defensive, and 2nd team All-NBA for 2017-18. JoJo is not only one of the most entertaining twitter follows, he is also on the cover of EA Sports NBA Live 19!

World B. Free – Sixers/G (1975-78, 1986-87) Lloyd "World B" Free was the 23rd overall selection in the 1975 NBA Draft. Free played his first three seasons with the Sixers and showed hints of the brilliance to come before demanding a trade out of Philly. He went on to play 886 NBA games, averaging 20.3 points per game and scoring a total of 17,955.

Did you know...

... Sixers star Joel Embiid is fluent in three languages (English, French, and Basaa).

... Flyers Don Gillen is the only Flyer to score a goal in his only game with the team.

Oddly enough...

21... The Flyers have been awarded penalty shots against 21 teams over their history. Their very first penalty shot was awarded to Bill Clement against the Detroit Red Wings on March 7th, 1974. It's the only penalty shot against the Red Wings in Flyers team history.

21... Flyers Ville Leino is tied for the NHL record for playoff points in a playoff season by a rookie, notching 21 points during the 2009-2010 NHL Playoffs.

22

Timmy Brown – Eagles/RB (1960-67) Timmy Brown was an all-purpose back with the Eagles and a member of the 1960 NFL Championship team. The three-time Pro Bowler had at least one 80+ yard reception three consecutive seasons. Brown amassed 7,049 yards from scrimmage over his eight seasons with the Birds (3,703 rush, 3,346 rec). Brown, a dynamic runner, also returned kick-offs for the Birds. His 105-yard kick return vs. Cleveland to open the 1961 season is still the 2nd longest in team history (Josh Huff). On November 6th, 1966 vs. Dallas Cowboys, Brown returned an NFL record two kick-offs for touchdowns (93yd and 90 yd). Brown was named to the NFLs 1960s All-Decade Team, the Eagles 75th Anniversary Team, and entered the Eagles Hall of Fame in 1990.

Rick Tocchet – Flyers/RW (1984-92, 2000-02) Rick Tocchet was a proto-typical power forward who helped power the Flyers to two Stanley Cup Finals in the mid-1980s. Widely regarded as one of the top-20 power forwards of all-time, Tocchet was a four-time 30+ goal scorer for the orange and black. He scored 96 points for the team in 1989-90 and is one of only three NHLers to amass 400 goals and 2000 PIMs. Tocchet had two stints with the Flyers and had a team record 9 Gordie Howe Hat tricks. He's the NHL's all-time leader with 18 Gordie Howe hat tricks. While GHHTs are not an official NHL stat, it shows Tocchet's formidability on the ice. The four-time All Star scored 232 goals and 508 points for the flyers in 621 games.

Andrew Toney – Sixers/G (1980-88) Andrew Toney played his entire career for the Sixers and was a member of their 1983 NBA Championship team. Toney was dubbed "the Boston Strangler" by Boston media during the Sixers/Celtics rivalry of the 1980s for his ability to dominate games. The two-time NBA All Star finished with 7,458 career points. Toney ranks 9th all-time on Sixers 2pt FG% percentage list. Chronic foot injuries cut short a possible Hall of Fame career.

Asante Samuel – Eagles/CB (2008-11) Asante Samuel was an interception machine during his four years with the Eagles. Samuel went to three Pro Bowls during his time with the Birds, and was 2nd Team All Pro in 2009. While with the Eagles, Samuel led the NFL with 9 INTs in 2009 (tied for 2nd on Eagles All-time list) and led the NFC with 7 INTs in 2010. Samuel had 51 INTs over his 11-year NFL Career. Samuel had 23 INTs in his four-year stint with the Birds, running two of them back for TDs. He also ran an INT back for a TD in the 2009 playoffs.

Did you know…

… Eagles Hall of Fame RB Timmy Brown turned to acting after his playing days and is one of only four people to appear in both the movie and TV version of M.A.S.H.

… Eagles RB Duce Staley had a team record 262 yards from scrimmage vs. Dallas Cowboys on September 3rd, 2000.

Even up...

22... Brett Brown became the 22nd Head Coach in Sixers history when the team hired him in 2013.

22... Eagles kicker Alex Henery kicked a team-record 22 consecutive successful FGs in 2012.

22... On April 14th, 2005, the Sixers scored a team-record 22 points in overtime in a 126-119 victory over the Miami Heat.

23

Troy Vincent – Eagles/CB (1996-03) Troy Vincent spent 8 seasons with the Eagles. The five-time Pro Bowler and three-time All-Pro was the NFL INT leader (tied) in 1999. Off the field, Troy Vincent is well-known for his humanitarian and charity work. Vincent won the Walter Payton Man-of-the-Year Award and the "Whizzer" White NFL Man-of-the-Year Award in 2002, and the Bart Starr Man-of-the-Year Award in 2004. Vincent was selected to the Eagles 75th Anniversary Team in 2007 and entered the Eagles Hall of Fame in 2012. Vincent is currently the NFL Executive VP of Football Operations.

Ilkka Sinisalo – Flyers/RW (1982-90) The Finish winger was a staple of the Flyers teams in the 1980's that twice went to the Stanley Cup Finals. Sinisalo spent nine seasons with the orange and black scoring 20+ goals in a season six times, and having two 30+ goal seasons. Ilkka ScoraGoala is the 3rd highest European scorer in team history. Among Finnish players to play in the NHL, Sinisalo ranks 7th all-time in goals scored (204), 15th in points (427), 4th in plus/minus (+126), 4th in short-handed goals (12), and 3rd in goals per game with 0.351 (200 NHL games min). Sinisalo was elected to the Finnish Hockey Hall of Fame in 1997. Sinisalo passed away in 2017.

Did you know...

... Phillies CF Oscar Gamble had the last hit at Connie Mack Stadium, a 10th inning single that scored Tim McCarver giving the Phillies a walk-off 2-1 win over the Montreal Expos on October 1st, 1970.

... Flyers Ilkka Sinisalo is one of only five NHLers to score their first career NHL goal on a penalty shot.

... On November 3rd, 1996 in Dallas, in the game's closing seconds, Eagles James Willis intercepted a Troy Aikman pass four yards deep in the end zone, ran it out to the 10 yard line and tossed a lateral to teammate Troy Vincent who ran 90 yards for the TD to preserve the win. The 104-yard TD is the longest INT in team history.

Oddly enough...

23... Eagles great Pete Retzlaff had a team-record 23 100-yard receiving games during his Eagles career.

23... On May 17th, 1979, the Phillies scored 23 runs in a 23-22 win over the Chicago Cubs. Mike Schmidt homered in the top of the 10th and the Phillies held on to win. It was the second time the Phillies had scored 23 against the Cubs. On August 25th, 1922, the Cubs beat the Phillies 26-23 in the highest scoring game in MLB history (49 total runs).

24

Mike Lieberthal – Phillies/C (1994-06) Mike Lieberthal was one of the greatest catchers to ever wear a Phillies uniform. Lieby was a two-time NL All Star, and a 1999 Gold Glover. Lieberthal is the all-time team leader in games caught with 1,139. He became only the third Phillies catcher to appear in an All Star game (1999). Lieberthal became the fourth catcher in MLB history to hit 30 HRs the same year he won the Gold Glove (1999), and just the 8th catcher in league history to hit 30 HRs and hit .300 in the same season. Lieberthal won the NL Comeback Player of the Year Award in 2002. He caught Kevin Millwood's 2003 no-hitter. The Phillies made the post season the year before Lieberthal joined the team, and again the year after he left. Lieberthal never made the post season during his 13-year MLB career. He entered the Phillies Wall of Fame in 2012.

Bobby Jones – Sixers/F (1978-86) Bobby Jones was a defensive stalwart for eight seasons with the Sixers. Jones, a member of the Sixers 1983 NBA Championship team, was a four-time NBA All Star, eight-time NBA All Defensive 1st Team, and won the NBA's 1st ever Sixth Man Award in 1983. Jones was on the infamous Silver medal-winning 1972 US Men's Basketball Team that lost the controversial Gold Medal game to the Soviet Union at the Munich Olympics. The Sixers retired his #24 in 1986.

Sami Kapanen – Flyers/RW (2003-08) Speedy Sami Kapanen was a fan favorite in the orange and black for 5 seasons. Prior to his stay in Philly, Kapanen, a two-time NHL All Star, won the Fastest Skater skills competition twice. Kapanen won two bronze medals with the Finnish Men's Hockey Team at 1994 and 1998 Winter Olympics. Kapanen won the Yanick Dupre Award in 2004 and the Gene Hart Memorial Award in 2007.

Did you know...

... Phillies catcher Mike Lieberthal's bobblehead appeared frequently on the TV show The Office.

... During his professional career, Sixers great Bobby Jones was never on a non-playoff team.

Even up...

24... Doug Pederson became the 24th Head Coach in Eagles history when he was hired for the 2016 season.

25

Tommy McDonald – Eagles/WR (1957-63) Tommy McDonald was a Flanker for the Eagles in the pre-Super Bowl era. He was a member of the 1960 NFL Championship team. McDonald played seven seasons for the Birds, and though he's ranked 32nd for the Eagles all-time in games played by a receiver, he's 2nd all-time in receiving TDs with 66. On October 4th, 1959 vs. New York Giants, Tommy scored four touchdowns (tied for team record). On December 10th, 1961 vs. New York Giants, McDonald had 237 receiving yards (Eagles team record). His 5,499 receiving yards ranks 6th best in team history. During his time with the Eagles, McDonald went to five Pro Bowls, was 1st Team All Pro twice, 2nd Team All Pro twice, led NFL in receiving yards in 1961, and twice led the league in receiving TDs. He was voted to the 75th Anniversary Team, entered the Eagles Hall of Fame in 1988, and the Pro Football Hall of Fame in 1998.

Chet Walker – Sixers/F (1962-69) Chet the Jet was a member of the 1967 Sixers NBA Championship team, widely regarded as one of the absolute best teams in NBA history. He was a 1st Team All-Rookie in 1963 and went to three NBA All Star games as a Sixer. Walker's .859 free throw % led the NBA in 1970-71. Walker ranks in the top 100 all-time in minutes played, FG, FGA, and just about every other offensive statistical category. Walker entered the Sixers Hall of Fame in 2012 and the NBA Hall of Fame in 2012.

Keith Primeau – Flyers/C (2000-06) Keith Primeau was a power center who spent 6 seasons with the Flyers. Primeau scored 12 goals in 58 playoff games with the Flyers but none bigger than the goal he scored on May 5th, 2000. Preems scored 12:01 into the 5th overtime period (152:01) beating Penguins goaltender Ron Tugnutt with a wicked wrister to end the 3rd longest NHL playoff game and the longest since the 1930s. Primeau was the 12th Flyer to wear the "C" and was a 2004 NHL All Star. Primeau won the Yanick Dupre Award in 2001, and the Toyota Cup in 2003. Primeau's stellar career was ended prematurely in 2006 due to post-concussion syndrome.

LeSean McCoy - Eagles/RB (2009-14) LeSean "Shady" McCoy spent six seasons in Midnight Green and was one of the Bird's most dominant RBs ever. During his time in Philly, McCoy went to three Pro Bowls, was 1st Team All Pro twice, NFL Rushing leader in 2013, NFL rushing TDs leader in 2011, and won the FedEx Ground Player of the Year Award in 2011. He is the team's all-time leading rusher with 6,792 yards. He had four 1,000-yard seasons, twice scored three TDs in one game, and had a team-record 9 consecutive games TD scoring streak. His single season team records include 20 TDs in 2011, and 1,607 rushing yards in 2013. On December 8th, 2013 vs. Detroit Lions in a snowy game, Shady rushed for a team record 217 yards.

Jim Thome – Phillies/1B (2003-2005, 2012) Class Guy Jim Thome was a prolific power hitter whose 612 career HRs puts him 8th all-time in MLB history. Thome had two stints with the Phillies, most notably in 2003 when he led the NL with 47 HRs, and in 2004 when he pounded another 42, was an NL All Star, NL Player of the Month for June, was the Players Choice MLB Man of the Year and Lou Gehrig Memorial Award winner. Thome's career accomplishments include being one of only four major leaguers to hit 100+ HRs with three different teams (Phillies, Chicago White Sox, Cleveland Indians), 19th best career OPS at .956, 26th all-time in RBIs with 1,699, and more walk-off HRs (13) than anyone else in the modern era of baseball. Thome finished with 2,328 career hits and hit 40 or more HRs 6 times. Thome entered the Phillies Wall of Fame in 2016, and was a first ballot Baseball Hall of Fame inductee in 2018.

Ben Simmons – Sixers/G/F (2016-present) Simmons started his NBA career in impressive fashion. He joined legendary Oscar Robertson as the only two NBA players with 10+ points, 10+ rebounds, and 5+ assists in each of their first three games. He is also only the third player in NBA history to record a triple double in his first four games. He then became the only player in NBA history to average 17 points, 10 rebounds, and 8 assists in his first ten games. He also broke Allen Iverson's Sixer rookie assist record. Simmons finished the season with 11 triple doubles, 3rd best in the league. Simmons was named NBA Rookie of the Year for 2017-18.

Did you know...

... LeSean McCoy is one of three Eagle running backs to come out of Bishop McDevitt HS in Harrisburg, Pa. (Larry Conjar played for the Eagles in 1968, and Ricky Watters played for the Eagles 1995-97).

... Eagles Tommy MacDonald was the last player in the NFL to play without a face mask (not including kickers).

... Sixers Hall of Famer Chet Walker was on an episode of the TV show The White Shadow in 1980.

... On April 21st, 2018, Sixers rookie Ben Simmons became just the 5th NBA rookie to ever have a triple double in an NBA playoff game, in a 106-102 game 4 win over the Miami Heat (Magic Johnson, Kareem Abdul-Jabbar, Jerry Lucas, and Tom Gola).

... Sixers Ben Simmons was born in Melbourne, Australia.

Oddly enough...

25... The Sixers had 25 consecutive home wins from December 17th, 1977 to April 5th, 1978.

25... The Eagles won Super Bowl LII in 2018. It was the 25th season the Eagles had made the playoffs.

25... In 1977, Phillies infielder Ted Sizemore ground into a team record-tying 25 double plays (Del Ennis 1950).

26

Chase Utley – Phillies/2B (2002-15) Chase "the Man" Utley was the greatest second baseman in team history. A fixture throughout the greatest era in Phillies baseball, Utley led the Phils to a World Series Championship in 2008. His 7 career World Series HRs is the most ever for a second baseman. The six-time NL All Star and four-time Silver Slugger was named to Sports Illustrated 2000's All-Decade Team. Utley won the Mike Schmidt MVP Award in 2005. His 35-game hitting streak in 2006 was tied for the longest ever by a second baseman. While Utley was good at hitting the ball, the ball was good at hitting Utley as evidenced by his team record 173 career HBPs.

Following the Phillies 2008 World Series Victory Parade, the soft-spoken Utley stunned the crowd gathered at Citizen's Bank Park when he infamously shouted on live TV "World F**king Champions!"

Brian Propp – Flyers/LW (1980-90) Brian Propp was a dominant winger for the Flyers' teams that went to the Stanley Cup Finals in 1980, 1985, and 1987, and had the NHL record 35-game unbeaten streak. Propp, known for his trademark "guffaw," scored the game-winning goal vs. New York Islanders (Billy Smith) in his NHL debut. Propper, a five-time All Star is 2nd all-time in Flyers goal scoring with 369 (Bill Barber), and assists with 480 (Bob Clarke), and 3rd in games played (790) and points (849) behind Clarke and Barber. Propp's 356 goals in the 1980s were second most by a left winger. His 75 points in 1979-80 were an NHL record for a rookie LW (since broken). Propp holds the Flyers team season record for Game-winning goals (12), and short-handed goals (7 tied). He holds the NHL record for most career playoff assists by a LW (84), most career playoff points by a LW (148), and most career playoff power play goals by a LW (27). Propp was linemates with Mario Lemieux and Wayne Gretzky for Gold Medal-winning Team Canada at the 1987 Canada Cup. Propp entered the Flyers Hall of Fame in 1999.

Lito Sheppard – Eagles/CB (2002-08) Defensive Back Lito Sheppard was a 1st round pick by the Eagles in the 2002 NFL Draft. He was a member of the 2004 NFC Championship Team that played the New England Patriots in Super Bowl XXXIX. Sheppard was a two-time Pro Bowler and 1st Team All-Pro in 2004. Between 2003 and 2007 Sheppard had 65 passes defended, 17 INTs, 460 INT return yards, and three INT TDs, including a 101-yard INT return vs. Dallas Cowboys 11/15/2004, and a 102-yard INT return vs. Dallas Cowboys on 10/8/2006. Sheppard was both a high school and college All-American.

Did you know...

... Chase Utley's first career MLB hit was a Grand Slam HR off Aaron Cook on April 24th, 2003 vs. Colorado Rockies. The rightfielder for the Rockies who watched it clear the fence over his head was current Phillies Manager Gabe Kapler.

... Chase Utley recorded the last-ever out at Veterans Stadium, hitting into a double play to end the game on September 28th, 2003 vs. Atlanta Braves.

Even up...

26... On November 19th 1978, Herman Edwards returned a 26 yard Joe Pisarcik fumble recovery for a TD in the game's waning moments for a come-from-behind 19-17 win over the New York Giants. The play, known as The Miracle of the Meadowlands changed the way NFL teams run out the clock to ensure wins.

26... The Eagles have selected 26 players from Notre Dame in the NFL Draft, the most from any college. DT Trevor Laws in the 2nd round of 2008 was the most recent. They have only selected three from Notre Dame since they selected Allen Rossum in the 3rd round 20 years ago (Laws-2008 2nd round, Victor Abiamiri DE 2007 2nd round, Tyreo Harrison LB 2002 6th round).

Even up...

26... On June 11th, 1985 the Phillies scored a team-record 26 runs against the New York Mets at the Vet in a 26-7 win.

26... There have been 26 Jackson's on the big four sports teams (7-Phillies, 15-Eagles, 4-Sixers). The only Jackson the Flyers have had is their voice, Jim Jackson.

26... Eagles defensive coordinator Jim Johnson sent Eagles to the Pro Bowl 26 times: Brian Dawkins (7), Troy Vincent (5), Jeremiah Trotter (4), Hugh Douglas (3), Lito Sheppard (2), Trent Cole, Michael Lewis, Asante Samuel, Corey Simon, and Bobby Taylor (1).

26... Sixers players have had 50+ points in a single game 26 times. Wilt Chamberlain had a team-record eleven 50+ point games, Allen Iverson had ten, and one each for Willie Burton, Moses Malone, Dana Barros, Hal Greer, and Dolph Schayes.

27

Ron Hextall – Flyers/G (player 1987-92 1994-99, GM 2014-2018) Ron Hextall was one of the greatest goaltenders in Flyers' team history. Hexy was the third-generation Hextall to play in the NHL. His father and uncle both played more than a decade in the league, and his grandfather is in the Hall of Fame. With that kind of lineage it's no surprise Hextall made his mark on the game. He revolutionized the position with his toughness and superior puck-handling skills, often acting like a sixth skater. Hextall was the first goalie in NHL history to shoot the puck into the opposition net, doing so on December 8th, 1987. Hexy did it again during the following year's playoffs, scoring into the net against the Washington Capitals on April 11th, 1989. Five other goaltenders have since shot the puck into the opposition net, but Hextall is the only goalie with two.

Hextall started his NHL career in 1986-87 and led the Flyers to the Stanley Cup Finals. Hexy finished 2nd in Calder Trophy voting, won the Vezina Trophy, and became just the 4th player ever to win the Conn Smythe Award as MVP of the Stanley Cup playoffs for a non-Cup winning team. Hextall also appeared in the 1997 Stanley Cup Finals with the Flyers. Hextall is the Flyers all-time goaltending leader in games played (489), wins (240), points scored (28), and PIMs (476). Hexy entered the Flyers Hall of Fame in 2008.

Reggie Leach – Flyers/RW (1975-82) The Riverton Rifle, Reggie Leach was a member of the famed LCB line (Leach, Clarke, Barber) leading the Flyers to their second Stanley Cup in 1975. In 1976, as the Flyers tried to win their third Cup in a row, Leach had a record-breaking 61 goals during the regular season (still a Flyers record), and a record 19 goals in the playoffs. Leach also tied an NHL playoff record scoring 5 goals in one game, doing so against the Boston Bruins. Leach, despite being on the losing end of the Stanley Cup Finals in 1976, won the Conn Smythe Trophy as MVP of the playoffs, the only non-goalie non-Cup winner to ever do so. Leach, a two-time NHL All Star was also a member of the Flyers 35-game unbeaten streak team. Leach entered the Flyers Hall of Fame in 1992.

Malcolm Jenkins – Eagles/S (2014-present) Malcolm Jenkins is the Eagles leader of the defensive backfield. From 2014 to 2017, Jenkins had four pick sixes, one of which was for 99 yards. He also had 201 solo tackles over that time and did not miss a single game. Jenkins won the 2017 "Whizzer" White NFL Man of the Year award and was named to his 2nd Pro Bowl. He was an important part of the Eagles drive to their Super Bowl LII Championship.

Aaron Nola – Phillies/P (2015-present) Nola was selected 7th overall by the Phillies in the 2014 MLB Amateur Draft. He made his MLB debut just 406 days after signing with the Phils. Nola had an RBI single in his 1st big league win, an 11-5 victory over the Chicago Cubs on July 26th, 2015. Nola was named the Phillies opening day starter for 2018 by first-year Phillies Manager Gabe Kapler, and finished as the Phils Ace going 17-6.

Placido Polanco – Phillies/INF (2002-05, 2010-12) Placido Polanco was a versatile infielder who enjoyed two stints in Philly. Polanco's first go-around with the Phils saw him predominantly a second baseman. He was traded away in June of 2005 to make room for Chase Utley. When Polanco returned to the team in 2010 he was at third base. Polanco was an NL All Star and Gold Glover in 2011. Though Polanco finished his playing career with the Miami Marlins, he officially retired as a Phillie on August 14th, 2016.

Kent Tekulve – Phillies/P (1985-88) Kent Tekulve was a submarine-throwing bullpen workhorse who pitched for the Phillies in the mid to late 1980s. Tekulve led the majors in games pitched four times, and appeared in 90+ games an MLB record three times. In 1987, 40-year old Teke became the oldest pitcher in league history to appear in 90 games. In August of 1987 Tekulve pitched in a game an MLB record 9 consecutive days. Tekulve also holds the MLB record for most career losses in games he yielded no earned runs (12). Tekulve was part of the Phillies broadcast team from 1991-97. On September 5th, 2014 Tekulve underwent successful heart transplant surgery. He officially retired from broadcasting in 2017.

Quintin Mikell – Eagles/S (2003-10) Quintin Mikell was a member of the 2004 Eagles team that went to Super Bowl XXXIX. He was a 2009 Pro Bowler and a 2nd team All Pro in 2008 and 2010. Mikell had 35 special teams tackles in 2006 and was the Eagles special teams MVP in 2005 and 2006. On October 23rd, 2005 vs. San Diego Chargers, Mikell blocked a

FG that teammate Matt Ware returned 65 yards for a TD. It was the first blocked FG returned for a TD in team history.

Willie Montanez – Phillies/1B (1970-75, 1982) Guillermo "Willie" Montanez served two stints in Phillies pinstripes. He holds the Phillies rookie record with 30 HRs in 1971, along with 99 RBIs and a National League leading 13 sac flies. He was 2nd in Rookie of the Year voting. Montanez led the NL in doubles in 1972. The flashy Montanez was known for his quick bat flip. Montanez was eventually traded for a huge piece to the Phillies World Series puzzle, the "Secretary of Defense" Garry Maddox. Over 13 MLB seasons, Montanez finished with 802 RBIs.

Did you know...

... To date, no Sixer has ever worn the #27. But 17 Flyers, 40 Phillies, and 31 Eagles have.

... Reggie Leach scored 19 goals in the 1975-76 NHL Stanley Cup Playoffs earning him the league's Conn Smythe Trophy as MVP of the playoffs. Leach remains the only non-goalie to win the award for a non-Cup winning team.

... On May 6th, 1976, Flyer winger Reggie Leach scored 5 goals against the Boston Bruins in a playoff game giving the Flyers a 6-3 win and closing out the Bruins 4 games to 1. The Flyers went on to their 3rd consecutive Stanley Cup Final but lost to the Montreal Canadiens. Leach's 5-goal game is the only one in team history.

... Flyers goalie Ron Hextall once left the goal crease in the waning moments of their playoff season to attack Montreal Canadiens Chris Chelios after Chelios had knocked Brian Propp out of the playoffs earlier in the series with a vicious elbow to the head. Hextall received a 15-game suspension.

Ouch... Phillies great Chase Utley was hit by pitches a team-record 27 times in 2008, breaking his own record of 25 set the season prior.

28

Claude Giroux – Flyers/C-LW (2008-present) Claude Giroux has been a dynamic piece of the Flyers puzzle for the last decade. Through the 2018 season, Giroux has been a 25+ goal and 70+ point scorer five times. He has 65 career playoff points in 69 career playoff games. He finished 2nd in the league in scoring in 2018, and 3rd in the league in scoring in 2012 and 2014. Giroux scored a team record 6 points in a playoff game vs. Pittsburgh Penguins on April 13th, 2012 (3g 3a). Giroux, a six-time All Star, finished 4th in the NHL's Hart Trophy voting in 2012 and 2018, and 3rd in 2014. He won the Gene Hart Memorial Trophy in 2011, the Bobby Clarke Trophy in 2011, '12, '14, '16, and '18, and the Toyota Cup in 2012-16 and 2018. Giroux was named the 19th captain in team history on January 13th, 2013 prior to the start of the lockout-shortened 2012-13 season. Giroux scored his 200th goal on February 18th, 2018 vs New York Rangers (Henrik Lundqvist). Giroux was a 2nd team NHL All Star for the 2017-18 season, and a 2018-19 Eastern Conference All Star.

Bill Bradley – Eagles/S (1969-76) Bill Bradley was a versatile defensive standout for the Birds in the early 1970s. Bradley was a DB, punter, and punt/kick returner over his Eagles career. Bradley was a three-time Pro Bowler and a two-time 1st Team All Pro. Bradley led the NFL in INTs in 1971 (11) and 1972 (9), and was the first player to ever lead the league in INTs in consecutive seasons. He is the Eagles career INT leader (34 tied w/ Brian Dawkins and Eric Allen), and holds the Eagles team record for INT return yards in a season (249), and career (536). Bradley entered the Eagles Hall of Fame in 1993.

Mitch Williams – Phillies/P (1991-93) Mitch Williams was a hard-throwing relief pitcher and a member of the 1993 Phillies team that went to the World Series. "Wild Thing" had a propensity for control issues walking 170 batters over 231.1 innings with the Phillies. His high walk counts aside, Mitchie-poo was 6th in Cy Young voting for 1991, and had 43 saves in 1993. He is the Phillies all-time lefty saves leader with 102. Williams is best remembered in Philly for the walk-off homer he gave up to Joe Carter in game six of the 1993 World Series ending the Phillies magical run.

Jayson Werth – Phillies/OF (2007-10)   Jayson Werth was a member of the Phillies 2008 World Series Champions. Werth hit 95 HRs and 300 RBIs in his four seasons with the Phils and was a 2009 NL All Star. On May 16th, 2008, vs Toronto Blue Jays, Werth hit three HRs (a grand slam, a 3-run hr and a solo shot) for 8 RBIs, tying a Phillies record. On May 12th, 2009, vs. Los Angeles Dodgers, Werth stole 2nd base, 3rd base, and then with the bases loaded, stole home. He finished the night with a team record-tying 4 stolen bases. In 2008, Werth led all MLB in HRs vs. lefties with 16. He was a 2009 NL All Star.

Raul Ibanez – Phillies/OF (2009-11) Class guy Raul Ibanez spent three seasons in Philadelphia and played on the 2009 team that lost in the World Series to the Yankees. Ibanez hit 34 HRs (career high) and 93 RBIs in 2009, his first year with the Phils. He was NL Player of the week 5 times that season was selected for his first and only All Star game of his 19-year MLB career. Ibanez hit 70 HRs and 260 RBIs over three seasons in Phillies pinstripes. Prior to his stint with the Phillies, Ibanez once went 6 for 6 with six singles in a game vs California Angels. It was the first time in 42 years a player had six hits in a game and all were singles. Ibanez was once voted by his peers the 2nd nicest guy in baseball, behind Jim Thome.

Kjell Samuelsson – Flyers/D (1986-92, 1995-98) Kjell Samuelsson was a giant on the Flyers blueline. At 6 feet 6 inches and 235 lbs, he was the largest player to don the orange and black during the 20th Century. Samuelsson played 9 seasons with the Flyers, his best coming in the 1997-98 campaign when he had a career high 30 points and a +28 and was selected to the 1998 All Star game. Samuelsson finished his Flyers' career with 545 games played, 35g 106a 141pts and a +103.

Did you know...

... Twice in team history, the Flyers have had two 100-point scorers in the same season, 1972-73 (Bobby Clarke-104, Rick MacLeish-100), and 1975-76 (Bobby Clarke-119, Bill Barber-112).

... Flyers captain Claude Giroux was featured on the cover of the EA Sports video game, NHL 13.

... On October 8th, 2015 vs Tampa Bay Lightning, Claude Giroux and Scott Laughton were both awarded penalty shots. It's the only multiple penalty shot game the Flyers have had. Neither player scored.

... Flyers goalie Ron Hextall had 28 points during his Flyers career (1 goal 27 assists). Hexy added another goal and 4 assists in the playoffs.

... On April 7th, 2018, during the last game of the season, Flyers captain Claude Giroux had a hat trick against the New York Rangers, giving him 102 points for the season, ending the Flyers longest 100-point player drought in team history (Eric Lindros 115 pts 1995-96).

... Jayson Werth is one of only five 3rd-generation major leaguers. His grandfather Ducky Schofield, and uncle Dick Schofield were both World Series winners. The other four 3rd-generation families were the Boone's (Bret Boone was the 1st ever MLB third-gen player), the Bells, the Colemans, and the Hairstons.

... Phillies Wild Thing Mitch Williams wore #28 during the 1991 and 1992 seasons before changing to #99 in 1993.

29

Harold Jackson – Eagles/WR (1969-72) Harold Jackson played four seasons for the Birds and had two of the best seasons of any Eagles receivers. Jackson led the league in receiving yards in 1969 (1,116 yards) and 1972 (1,048 yards). Jackson was 2nd Team All Pro in 1972 and a Pro Bowler in 1969, and 1972.

John Kruk – Phillies/1B (1989-94) John Kruk was a fan favorite and a member of the 1993 Macho Row team that went to the World Series. Kruk was a three-time NL All Star with the Phils, and was voted to the Phillies All-Vet team (1971-93). In 1994, Kruk was diagnosed with testicular cancer. Kruk retired during the following season. In 1987, as a member of the San Diego Padres, Kruk, along with Marvell Wynn and Tony Gwynn became the only players in MLB history to open their 1st inning of a game with three consecutive HRs. Krukker is currently a member of the Phillies broadcast team. Kruk entered the Phillies Wall of Fame in 2011.

Did you know...

... Phillies slugger turned broadcaster John Kruk had a memorable moment in the 1993 MLB All Star game when a Randy Johnson fastball sailed over his head and hit the backstop. Kruk mimicked his racing heart by tapping his chest and blowing out deep breaths. He flailed at a third strike, just happy to get out of the at-bat alive.

... 21 Flyers have worn the #29 in team history. Ray Emery is the only goalie to wear it.

... Eagles career rushing leader LeSean McCoy wore the #29 during his rookie season in 2009. He switched to #25 for the 2010 season.

Oddly enough...

29... On October 20th, 1993 the Phillies lost game 4 of the 1993 World Series to the Toronto Blue Jays 15-14. The 29 total runs scored are the most for a World Series game in MLB history.

30

George McGinnis – Sixers/F (1975-78) George McGinnis was an integral part of the Sixers 1977 NBA Finals team. McGinnis averaged 20+ points in each season with the Sixers and was 5th in the league in points in 1975-76. McGinnis was an All Star twice with the Sixers, and was 1st Team All NBA in 1976 and 2nd Team All NBA in 1977. McGinnis entered the Basketball Hall of Fame in 2017.

Brian Mitchell – Eagles/PR-KR (2000-02) Brian Mitchell was one of the all-time greatest return specialists in NFL history. Mitchell is 2nd all-time in all-purpose yards in NFL history. He's the Eagles all-time leader in punt and kick returns despite only playing three seasons with the Birds. On November 25th, 2002 Mitchell had a 76-yard punt return TD vs San Francisco 49ers, becoming the NFL's all-time leader in punt return TDs with 13. He had six returns that game for 206 yards, also an NFL record. He also holds the NFL record for most combined yards vs a single opponent with 3,076 yards against the Dallas Cowboys. It's no wonder Mitchell was such a Philly fan favorite!

Antero Niittymaki – Flyers/G (2004-09) Antero Niittymaki was a popular goalie for the Flyers as much for his creative goalie mask as for his on-ice performance. Nitty came up through the Flyers system, winning the AHL's Calder Championship with the Philadelphia Phantoms in 2005 and being named the playoff MVP. On April 11, 2004, Nitty scored an AHL game-winning, empty-net, shorthanded goal for a 3-2 overtime win over the Hershey Bears. It's the only overtime goal by a goalie in North American pro hockey. On Jan 5th 2008 Niittymaki set a Flyers team record for saves in a game with 54 vs. Toronto Maple Leafs. Niittymaki also won a team record 16 straight games against the Atlanta Thrashers. Nitty won a silver medal with Team Finland at the 2006 Winter Olympics in Turin Italy. Niittymaki was named the MVP of the Olympic hockey tournament.

Dave Cash – Phillies/2B (1974-76) Dave Cash was a three-time All Star with the Phillies in the mid-70's. Cash led the NL in triples in 1976 with a career high 12. Cash also hit career highs with the Phillies in hits with 213 in 1975, RBIs with 58 in 1974, runs with 111 in 1975, walks with 56 in 1975 and HRs with 4 (yes, 4) in 1975.

Did you know…

… Flyers goalie Martin Houle's entire Flyers career spanned two minutes on the ice. He gave up one goal for a career Goals Against Average of 30.00.

… Flyers goalie and Mr. Universe Ilya Bryzgalov holds the Flyers team record for consecutive shutout minutes with 249:43 (March 8th, 2012 – March 15th, 2012).

Even up...

30... Flyers fan favorite Dan Briere holds the Flyers team record for single season playoff points when he notched 30 during the Flyers Stanley Cup Finals run in 2010.

30... Eagles Super Bowl XV QB Ron Jaworski was the 30th starting QB in team history.

30... On December 16th, 1967 Sixer great Wilt Chamberlain scored a team-record 30 FGs in a 143-123 victory over the Chicago Bulls.

31

Pelle Lindbergh – Flyers/G (1982-86) Pelle Lindbergh is among the top three goalies in Flyers team history. A tragic fatal car accident in November of 1985, just months after leading the Flyers to the Stanley Cup Finals, ended what many believe could have been a Hall of Fame career. Lindbergh was named to the NHL All-Rookie Team in 1983. In 1984-85 Lindbergh led the league with 40 wins and became the first European goaltender to win the NHL's Vezina Trophy for best goalie. Lindbergh was the first-ever recipient of the Bobby Clarke Trophy in 1985. Lindbergh was selected to three All Star games, the third in 1986 was posthumously. Beginning with the 1993-94 season the Flyers have annually awarded the Pelle Lindbergh Memorial Trophy to the team's most improved player.

Garry Maddox - Phillies/CF (1975-86) Garry Maddox was an 8-time Gold Glover and one of the game's greatest-fielding centerfielders. Legendary voice of the Phillies, Harry Kalas nicknamed Garry Maddox the Secretary of Defense. He also said of Maddox, "Two-thirds of the Earth is covered by water, the other third is covered by Garry Maddox." While Maddox was known for his defensive exploits, he had some success with the bat as well. Maddox drove in the winning run in the deciding game five of the NLCS in 1980 vs Houston Astros, and then caught the final out sending the Phillies to the World Series vs Kansas City Royals. In 1973, Maddox finished 3rd in hitting (.319 avg) and 2nd in triples (10). In 1976, Maddox again finished 3rd in hitting (.330 avg), and finished 3rd in doubles (37). The fleet-footed Maddox stole 20+ bases 9 consecutive seasons. Maddox won the World Series with the Phils in 1980, won the Roberto Clemente Award in 1986 and entered the Phillies Wall of Fame in 2001.

Wilbert Montgomery – Eagles/RB (1977-84) One of the most dynamic backs of his era, Wilbert Montgomery still holds several Eagle rushing records. He had a team record eight 100-yard rushing games in 1981, a team record 4 TDs in a game (tied w 5 others) and a team record 26 100-yard rushing games in his Eagles career. Montgomery was a Pro Bowler and 1st Team All-Pro for both the 1978 and 1979 seasons. Montgomery led the NFL with 2,012 all-purpose yards in 1979. Montgomery entered the Eagles Hall of Fame in 1987.

Jalen Mills – Eagles/CB (2016-Present) Jalen Mills celebrated coming to the Eagles by dyeing his hair neon green. Nicknamed the Green Goblin, Mills has 125 tackles, 21 pass deflections, 3 INTs in his two seasons with the Birds. On October 29th, 2017, Green Goblin intercepted a C.J. Beathard pass and ran 37 yards for a pick six vs San Francisco 49ers earning Mills NFC Defensive Player of the Week honors. Mills had 13 tackles in the 2017 playoffs including 9 vs New England Patriots in Super Bowl LII, helping the Birds win their first Super Bowl Championship in team history.

Did you know...

... Flyers goalie Pelle Lindbergh was the only goalie that played against the 1980 US Olympic gold medal-winning men's hockey team to not lose to them. His Team Sweden played the US team to a 2-2 tie in the tournament's opening game.

... Of the 6 Eagles who share the record for four TDs in a game, Wilbert Montgomery is the only Eagle to do it twice. He did it in 1978 and 1979 both against the Washington Redskins.

... Eagles great Wilbert Montgomery had a team-record 26 career 100-yard rushing games. He had 8 in 1981, also a team record.

... On July 21st, 1973, Phillies pitcher Ken Brett gave up Hank Aaron's 700th career home run in a Phillies 8-3 win in Atlanta.

... Garry Maddox won 8 Gold Glove Awards for the Phillies. In the team's history, only Mike Schmidt (10) had more.

... On June 2nd, 2002, Phillies P Robert Person hit a Grand Slam in the 1st inning and a 3-run homer in the 5th inning of an 18-3 Phillies home win over the Montreal Expos. Person nearly had a 2nd Grand Slam but the ball was just foul. Person had two homers and 7 RBIs for the day and recorded his 1st win of the season. Those two homers were his only two hits of the season, and his last two hits as a Phillie.

Oddly enough...

31... The Eagles and Houston Oilers combined for an Eagles-record 31 penalties On October 2nd, 1988. The Eagles were whistled for 19 of them in a 32-23 win.

31... There have been 31 Brown's on the big four sports teams, Byron, Earl, and George Browne notwithstanding... (7-Phillies, 17-Eagles, 2-Flyers, 5-Sixers).

31... Sixer great Wilt Chamberlain had 31 40+ point games during his Sixers career, 2nd-most in team history (Allen Iverson 76).

32

Steve Carlton – Phillies/P (1972-86) Steve Carlton was one of the game's all-time greatest hurlers. Lefty was a four-time Cy Young Award winner with the Phils. His 329 wins are 2nd all-time for lefties (Warren Spahn 363) and 4th best overall of the modern era. Carlton led the NL in wins four times, was the NL ERA leader in 1972, a Gold Glover in 1981 and led the NL in KOs 5 times. Carlton was a seven-time NL All Star with the Phillies, and in 1980 was 2-0 vs the Kansas City Royals helping the Phillies to their first World Series win. Carlton's 4,136 KOs in 2nd all-time for lefties. Carlton was a five-time 20 game winner and started 35+ games ten times for the Phils. Carlton also picked off 144 runners over his career. That's 62 more pickoffs than second place (Jerry Koosman 82). Of all the amazing stats and feats of Lefty's phenomenal career, quite possibly the most impressive is Carlton posting 27 wins on a Phillies team that only won 59. Carlton's winning 45.8% of his team's wins is the highest percentage in 120 years and by far the best of the modern era. The Phillies retired Lefty's #32 and entered him in their Wall of Fame in 1989. He was inducted into the Baseball Hall of Fame in 1994. The Phillies honored Carlton with a statue outside Citizen's Bank Park in 2004.

Billy Cunningham – Sixers/F (1965-72, 1974-76 as a player 1977-85 as a coach) Billy Cunningham did it all during his NBA career. Player, coach, commentator, owner... there really was nothing he could not do. As a player, the Kangaroo Kid was a four-time NBA All Star, a three-time 1st

team ALL NBA, a 2nd team ALL NBA, All-Rookie 1st team, and an NBA champion in 1967. He was also named to the NBA's 50th Anniversary All-Time Team.   As a Head Coach with the Sixers, he went to the NBA Finals three times and won the NBA Championship in 1983. His .698 winning percentage is third highest all-time. Cunningham made four All Star game appearances as coach, and his Sixers never missed the postseason.   Cunningham is the fastest NBA coach to 300 wins and 400 wins. The Sixers retired his #32, and he entered the Sixers Hall of Fame in 1986. The Kangaroo Kid was also inducted into the Basketball Hall of Fame in 1986.

Ricky Watters – Eagles/RB (1995-97) Ricky "Running" Watters was a very productive back during his time with the Eagles. Watters rushed for 1,000+ yards and was top ten in the league in each of his three seasons with the Birds. He also caught 161 passes out of the backfield. He may have caught 162 had he not bailed on a pass to avoid getting hit in his Eagles debut vs. Tampa Bay Buccaneers. Watters came under scrutiny for the soft play to which he responded "For who? For what?" The comment did not sit well with Eagles fans nor, apparently, with Hall of Fame voters. Watters was, however, a 1st team All Pro and a Pro Bowler for the Eagles in 1995 and 1996.

Murray Craven – Flyers/C (1984-92) Murray Craven was a solid two-way forward and a member of the Flyers' 1985 and 1987 Stanley Cup Finals teams. Craven led the Flyers in points in 1987-88 with 76, was 4th in short-handed goals (4) 1991-92, and 10th in +/- (+45) 1984-85. Craven had two hat tricks for the orange and black, and scored on a penalty shot

12/23/90 vs Montreal Canadiens in 4-4 tie. Craven played eight seasons for the Flyers and finished with +101 in 523 games.

Roman Cechmanek – Flyers/G (2000-03) Roman Cechmanek was a light in the Flyers net that burned brightly but seemed to fizzle too soon. Cechmanek was drafted by the Flyers in 2000 and beat out Brian Boucher for the starting goalie slot 2000-01. Cechmanek was an NHL All Star and finished 2nd in the Vezina Trophy voting in his stellar rookie season. Oddly, though Cechmanek finished 2nd in Vezina voting among all goalies, he wasn't among the top 15 candidates for the Calder Trophy for Rookie of the Year, though four goalies were (Evgeni Nabokov, Roberto Luongo, Marty Turco, Brent Johnson). Cechmanek won the William M. Jennings Trophy with teammate Robert Esche (and Devils goalie Martin Brodeur) in 2002-03. Cechmanek is the Flyers' all-time leader in career goals against average with 1.96 and save pct. .923. and single season GAA 1.83 in 2002-03. His 20 shutouts are second only to Bernie Parent (50) in team history. Cechmanek ranks 5th on Flyers' win list with 92. Cechmanek won the Bobby Clarke Trophy in 2001, and 2003 and was the first-ever Flyer recipient of the Toyota Cup in 2001. Flyers broadcaster Jim Jackson coined the phrase "Cranium Carom" to describe Cechmanek's penchant for head-butting pucks into the corner. Checko is the only Flyer goalie to wear #32.

Did you know...

... Billy Cunningham's .698 winning pct. as Sixers Head Coach is second in team history only to Alex Hannum's .798 pct. Both men coached the Sixers to an NBA title. Cunningham's squad won its title in 1983, and Cunningham was a member of Hannum's NBA Championship winning team in 1967.

... Billy Cunningham was the first Sixer to score 50 points in a post-season game (4/1/70 vs. Milwaukee Bucks). Allen Iverson (3 times) is the only other Sixer to accomplish this feat.

... Billy Cunningham's retired Sixers #32 was worn by Charles Barkley during the 1991-92 season to honor Magic Johnson after his HIV-positive announcement.

... Ricky Watters appeared in the movie Any Given Sunday.

... Ricky Watters is one of only two NFL players to have a 1,000 rushing yard season with three different teams (Willis McGahee).

Even up...

32... Consecutive victories for the Flyers over the Los Angeles Kings from October 22nd, 1974 to February 5th, 1983.

32... Flyers Hall of Famer Bobby Clarke scored a team-record 32 shorthanded goals for the Flyers during his career.

32... Eagles kicker Cody Parkey holds the Eagles team rookie-record for FGs in a season with 32 in 2014.

33

Brian Boucher – Flyers/G (1999-02, 2009-11, 2013) Brian Boucher has had four stints with the Flyers organization, one of which was solely with the Phantoms. Boosh had a notable rookie season for the Flyers. He led the league with a 1.91 GAA, and was named to the 1999-00 NHL All Rookie team. Boucher was the winning goalie in the Flyers record five overtime playoff win over the Pittsburgh Penguins. In his second stint with the Flyers, Boucher was part of a three goalie tandem that kept alternating throughout the season due to injury. Boosh led the Flyers to an opening round 4-1 series win over the favored New Jersey Devils. Boosh was then injured in the next series against Boston, in which the Flyers came from a 0-3 deficit to win the series. Boosh appeared in two Stanley Cup Final games against the Chicago Black Hawks. The following season Boosh became the only goalie in NHL history to win two playoff games in a series while coming in relief.   Boosh rejoined the Flyers for a third time after the 2012-13 lockout ended in January 2013. Boosh sits 10th on the Flyers all-time wins list with 73. As a Phoenix Coyote, Boucher set the modern era shutout streak of 332:01 in 2003-04. Boucher is currently a local and national hockey broadcast analyst.

Cliff Lee – Phillies/P (2009, 2011-14) Cliff Lee had two stints with the Phillies. In 2009, Lee was the Phillies World Series Game 1 starter vs. New York Yankees. Lee pitched a complete game 6-1 win. He became the 1st pitcher in MLB history to pitch a complete game in the World Series with no earned runs, no BBs and 10 KOs. The Phillies went on to lose the Series to the Yankees in six games, 4-2. Cliff Lee had both Phillies win. Lee was traded in the offseason as the Phillies pursued Roy Halladay. Lee rejoined the Phillies as a free-agent signing in 2011 saying he never wanted to leave in the first place. In his 2nd stint with the Phillies, Lee was part of the Phantastic Phour (Lee, Halladay, Hamels, Oswalt), one of the best rotations ever put together. Lee was NL Pitcher of the Month for June 2011, going 5-0 with an era of 0.21. Lee led the NL with 6 shutouts in 2011, the most shutouts for a NL pitcher in 22 years. Lee was a two-time All Star for the Phillies.

Pete Peeters – Flyers/G (1979-82, 1990-91) Peeters had two stints with the Flyers, the first more memorable than the last. Peeters started his first full season with the Flyers by going 25 games (20-0-5) before suffering his first defeat. The Flyers 35-game unbeaten streak is still the longest streak in North American professional sports. Peeters was third in Calder voting for Rookie of the Year in 1980 behind Ray Bourque and Mike Foligno, and just ahead of teammate Brian Propp. Peeters was an NHL All Star in 1980, 1981.

Hersey Hawkins – Sixers/G (1988-93) Hersey Hawkins was an NBA All Rookie for the Sixers in 1989, and an NBA All Star in 1991. Hawkins had 9 steals in a game vs. Boston Celtics on January 25th, 1991, tied for 2nd most in Sixers history. Hawkins was a member of the bronze-winning USA men's basketball team at the 1988 Seoul Olympics.

Did you know...

... On May 6th, 2011, Phillies pitcher Cliff Lee struck out 16 batters vs. Atlanta Braves but lost 5-0.

... In June 2011, Phillies pitcher Cliff Lee went 5-0 and personally outscored his opponents, scoring two runs in those five games while only giving up one.

... Cliff Lee won the AL Cy Young Award with the Cleveland Indians in 2008. Roy Halladay with the Toronto Blue Jays finished 2nd in voting. Three years later they became teammates and part of the Phantastic Phour Phillies rotation.

... Pete Peeters had a 25-game unbeaten streak with the Flyers and a 31-game unbeaten streak with Boston. He is the only goalie with two such unbeaten streaks in NHL history.

... Flyers forward Riley Cote is the only non-goaltender to wear #33 for the orange and black. He wore #33 in 2006-07 before switching to #32 2007-10.

... Flyers goalie Brian Boucher's sprawling, twisting, backward arm save against New Jersey Devil Patrik Elias is now known around the league as "the Boosh."

Did you know...

... On May 11th, 2006, vs New York Mets, Phillies outfielder #33 Aaron Rowand made a stunning over the shoulder catch before crashing into the outfield fence and damaging his face. Rowand broke his nose, cheekbone and orbital bone. He also required 15 stitches. After surgery and 15 days on the DL, Rowand returned to the line-up and was given two standing ovations.

Oddly enough...

33... There have been 33 Williams's on the big four sports teams (7-Phillies, 18-Eagles, 2-Flyers, 6-Sixers).

33... Eagles QB Carson Wentz threw a team-record 33 TD passes in 2017 while limited to 13 games due to a season-ending knee injury.

34

Charles Barkley – Sixers/F (1984-92) Charles Barkley was a dominant "under-sized" power forward who played his first eight seasons with the Sixers. As a Sixer, Barkley was a 1995 NBA 1st team All-Rookie, 1987 NBA Rebound leader, four-time All NBA 1st team, three-time All NBA 2nd team, six-time NBA All Star, and the 1991 All Star MVP. On November 30th, 1988, Barkley had 41 points, 22 rebounds, 5 assists, and 6 steals. He is the first NBA player to accomplish this feat. He was 2nd in MVP voting in 1989-90, and was Sporting News Player of the Year. Barkley was part of the US Men's Olympic basketball "Dream Team" that won gold in Barcelona in 1992 and Atlanta in 1996. From his days as the "Mound Round of Rebound" to his days as Sir Charles, Barkley was a fierce competitor who excelled everywhere along the line and as such, was named one of the 50 greatest players of all time. Barkley had his #34 retired by the Sixers and entered the Sixers Hall of Fame in 2006. Barkley has twice been inducted into the Basketball Hall of Fame, as a player in 2006, and as a member of the "Dream Team" in 2010.

Roy Halladay – Phillies/P (2010-13) Roy "Doc" Halladay was a dominant power pitcher with a penchant for going deep into games. Doc spent the last four seasons of his stellar career with the Phillies. Halladay won 203 games in his career (108th all-time) and posted 2,117 KOs (69th all-time). In Halladay's first season with the Phillies, he became the first Phillies 20-game winner in 28 years posting a 21-10 record. One of those wins was Halladay's perfect game vs Florida Marlins on May 29th. He was NL Pitcher of the Month for July, was awarded the MLB Clutch Performer of the Year Award, MLB Heart and Hustle Award, MLB.com Starter of the Year, was MLB wins leader, 2010 NL All Star, and became one of only six MLB pitchers in history to win the Cy Young in both leagues when he was named the NL winner for 2010. On October 6th, 2010, Halladay threw the 2nd-ever postseason no-hitter (NLDS vs Cincinnati Reds) in his first-ever postseason start. He became the 1st pitcher in 37 years to throw two no-hitters in same season, and the first ever to throw a no-hitter AND a perfect game in the same season. His postseason no-hitter won the 2010 MLB.com Postseason Moment of the Year Award for 2010. Halladay followed up his 2010 performance with another All Star appearance in 2011, 2nd in Cy Young voting (Clayton Kershaw), and winning a 2011 ESPY. Halladay was inducted into the Baseball Hall of Fame in 2019 (1st-ballot eligible). Tragically, Halladay died on 11/7/2017 when the plane he was piloting crashed into the Gulf of Mexico.

Did you know...

... Sixers Charles Barkley had a career high 14.6 rebounds per game in 1986-87, becoming the shortest player (6'6") in NBA history to lead the league in rebounding.

... During Phillies pitcher Roy Halladay's postseason no-hitter vs. Cincinnati Reds in 2010, Halladay only walked a single batter. He completed the no-hitter in 104 pitches!

... Phillies pitcher Roy Halladay beat every team in Major League Baseball during his Hall of Fame career, except the Phillies.

... John Vanbiesbrouck spent two seasons with the Flyers (1998-99, 1999-00). As of the end of the 2016-17 NHL season, Beezer played more games (882) and had more wins (374) than any other US-born goalie in NHL history. He was inducted into the US Hockey Hall of Fame in 2007.

... On February 22nd, 2018, Flyers goalie Peter Mrazek won his first game as a Flyer defeating the Columbus Blue Jackets 2-1. It was the fourth different Flyer goalie to win a game in a two-week period (Brian Elliott, Michal Neuvirth, Alex Lyon).

Even up...

34... Eagles punter Donnie Jones kicked a team-record 34 punts inside the opponent's 20-yard line in 2014. He had 33 the season prior.

35

Cole Hamels – Phillies/P (2006-2015) Cole "Hollywood" Hamels was an important piece to the Phillies late 2000's dominance. Hamels was an NL All Star in 2007, 2011, and 2012. Hamels was both the NLCS and World Series MVP in 2008 en route to the Phillies 2008 World Series Championship. "Hollywood" also won the Babe Ruth Award in 2008. Hamels pitched a combined no-hitter vs. Atlanta Braves on September 1st, 2014. Hamels then pitched a no-hitter in his Phillies farewell game on July 25th, 2015 vs. Chicago Cubs, becoming only the 5th pitcher with a no-hitter and a combined no-hitter.

Pete Pihos – Eagles/TE-FB (1947-1955) Pete Pihos played his entire career with the Eagles helping them to back to back Championships in 1948 and 1949 and was inducted into the Pro Football Hall of Fame in 1970. Pihos appeared in the first-ever Pro Bowl in 1951, his 1st of six consecutive selections. Pihos was a six-time 1st Team All Pro, and led the NFL in receptions, receiving yards and receiving touchdowns in 1953. Pihos led the league in receptions and receiving yards in 1954 and 1955, as well. Pihos was named to the NFL's All Decade Team for the 1940s. Pihos missed just one game in his entire nine-year career. Pihos was part of the inaugural Eagles Hall of Fame class of 1987.

Bob Froese – Flyers/G (1983-86) Bob Froese was a member of the Flyers' 1985 Stanley Cup Finals team and shared the nets with Pelle Lindbergh. Froese went 12-0-1 to start his NHL and Flyers career which was an NHL record at the time. Following Lindbergh's tragic death in November 1985, Froese elevated his game and was named a 1986 NHL All Star, and won the William M Jennings Trophy with back-up Darren Jensen. Froese finished 2nd to John Vanbiesbrouck in the Vezina Trophy voting. Froese sits 5th on the Flyers' all-time goalie wins list with 92.

Wayne Stephenson – Flyers/G (1974-79) Wayne Stephenson joined the Flyers for the 1974-75 season to back-up Bernie Parent and was a member of the Flyers' 2nd Stanley Cup-winning team in 1975. Stephenson took over the Flyer net in the 75-76 season when legend Bernie Parent went down with a pinched nerve injury. Stephenson was the winning goalie of the famous Flyers-Soviets game where the Flyers handed the Russians their only defeat and Stephenson out-dueled legendary Russian goalie Vladislav Tretiak, 6-1. Stephenson was a 1976 and 1978 NHL All Star. His 93 career Flyers wins is 4th on their all-time list. Earlier in his career, Stephenson won a bronze medal with Team Canada in the 1968 Grenoble Olympics. Stephenson died of brain cancer in 2010.

Did you know...

... Flyers goalie Bob Froese is one of just 9 NHL goalies to record an assist in their NHL debut. Froese beat the Hartford Whalers 7-4 on January 8th, 1983. It was just the 2nd "all-Cooperall" game in NHL history.

... In 2011, three of the Phillies Phantastic Phour pitchers finished in the top five in Cy Young voting, Roy Halladay -2nd, Cliff Lee -3rd, Cole Hamels, 5th.

... Phillies pitcher Cole Hamels hit his 1st career home run on July 21st, 2012 off Matt Cain of the San Francisco Giants. Oddly enough, when Cain hit a homer off Hamels in the top of the same inning, it was the first homer Hamels had given up to an opposing pitcher. It's also the only time for either club that starting pitchers hit homers off each other in the same inning.

... On September 1st, 2014 four Phillies pitchers combined to throw a no-hitter vs Atlanta Braves. Hamels went 6 innings and got the win. Jake Diekman, Ken Giles, and Jonathan Papelbon each threw 1 no-hit inning.

Oddly enough...

35... The Flyers 35-game unbeaten streak is the longest unbeaten streak in North American Professional Sports. The Flyers went 25-0-10 during the streak beginning with October 14th, 1979 (Toronto Maple Leafs) to January 6th, 1980 (Buffalo Sabres). The streak ended with a 7-1 loss to the Minnesota North Stars on January 7th, 1980. The loss preceeding the streak was a 9-2 drubbing at the hands of the Atlanta Flames in the second game of the season.

35... On December 6th, 2015 the Eagles (5-7) defeated the New England Patriots (10-2) 35-28. During the game, the Eagles scored on a 24yd Najee Goode TD on a Chris Maragos punt block, a 99-yard Malcolm Jenkins pick six, and an 83-yard punt return TD by Darren Sproles.

35... Eagles kicker Caleb Sturgis had a team-record 35 FGs in 2016.

36

Robin Roberts – Phillies/P (1948-61) Robin Roberts was one of the greatest right-handed pitchers in Phillies history. Roberts was a seven-time All Star, four-time MLB Wins leader, and two-time MLB Strikeout leader. At the end of the Whiz Kids 1950 season the 23-year old Roberts started three games in the last 5 days including 4 IP Wednesday September 27th , 8 IP Thursday Sept 28th, and a 10-inning complete game win on Sunday October 1st, the last day of the season, to put the Phillies in the World Series vs. New York Yankees. It was Roberts' 20th win of the season, making him the Phillies 1st 20-game winner since Grover Cleveland Alexander in 1917. Roberts was a 20-game winner for the following five consecutive seasons. Roberts had his #36 retired by the Phillies in 1962, was inducted into the Baseball Hall of Fame in 1976, entered the Phillies Wall of Fame in 1978, was named to the Phillies All Centennial Team in 1983, and was honored with a statue outside Citizens Bank Park in 2004.

Brian Westbrook – Eagles/RB (2002-09) Brian Westbrook was one of the greatest running backs in team history. Westbrook set a team record with 90 receptions in 2007 on his way to his 1st Team All Pro selection. Westbrook was a two-time Pro Bowler who led all running backs in receptions with 73 in 2004. On November 27th, 2008 Westbrook had four touchdowns (RB) vs Arizona Cardinals to tie a team record. Westbrook entered the Eagles Hall of Fame in 2015.

Did you know...

... Legendary Phillies pitcher Robin Roberts once completed 28 consecutive starts including a 17-inning marathon vs. Boston Braves on September 6th, 1952. Roberts faced 71 batters during the 7-6 win, and earned his 23rd win of the season.

... Phillies hurler Robin Roberts is the only pitcher to beat the Braves team in all three cities they called home (Boston, Milwaukee, and Atlanta).

... For two games in 1981, Flyer's Hall of Famer Bobby Clarke did not have his customary #16 sweater. His sweater was stolen following a loss in Edmonton. The only available sweater the Flyers were traveling with was #36. Clarke donned the unfamiliar number for two games, 2/27/81 vs. Winnipeg Jets and 2/28/81 vs. Minnesota North Stars. The Flyers won both games.

... The Flyers are tied for the NHL record most home wins during a single season, winning 36 games at the Spectrum during the 1975-76 season. They only lost at home twice all season. The "Philly flu" was particularly rampant that season.

... In 2002 Eagles running back Brian Westbrook threw a TD pass to Todd Pinkston in a 44-13 rout of the Dallas Cowboys on September 22nd, 2002.

Even up...

36... The number of Flyers who have worn the # 15 in the team's history, including four players in 1999 alone (Mark Greig, Richard Park, Mike Maneluk, and Andrei Kovalenko).

36... The 1936 Eagles only scored 6 TDs in a 12-game season. Their 1-11 record and 51 total points scored are both all-time Eagles lows.

36... The Eagles have shut out their opponents 36 times in team history.

37

Eric Desjardins – Flyers/D (1995-06) Eric "Rico" Desjardins joined the Flyers on February 9th, 1995 as part of the trade with the Montreal Canadiens that brought John LeClair and Gilbert Dionne in exchange for Mark Recchi and a 1995 3rd round draft pick. He became a mainstay on the Flyers blueline winning the Barry Ashbee Award for the Flyers best defenseman a team-record seven times. Rico was a two-time All Star and a two-time 2nd team All Star. Rico became the 12th captain in team history during the 1999-2000 season replacing Eric Lindros. Desjardins won the Yanick Dupre Award in 1999. Rico is the 2nd leading scoring defenseman in team history behind Mark Howe. Desjardins entered the Flyers Hall of Fame in 2015.

Ruben Amaro jr. – Phillies/OF (1980-83 bat boy, 1992-93, 1996-98 as player, 1998-2008 as AGM, 2008-2015 as GM) Ruben Amaro jr. was born in Philly while his dad, Ruben Amaro sr. was a member of the Phillies. Amaro jr. became a Phillies bat boy at the age of 15 (his father was 1st base coach). Twelve years later Amaro jr. was in the Phillies outfield. Amaro jr. spent 5 seasons with the Phillies before going on to serve as AGM, and GM during his Phillies career. Amaro jr.'s highlight during his playing career was batting .316 in 61 games in 1996. Amaro jr. played in 126 games for the Phils in 1992, and 117 in 1997 before moving into the front office following the 1998 season. While Amaro jr. was mostly a bench player for the Phils, he finished 3rd in HBP (9) in 1992, and had only

5 errors in 326 games in the OF. Amaro jr. won the 1980 World Series with the Phils, and was AGM when they won it again in 2008. Fans voted Amaro jr. MLB "This Year in Baseball" Executive of the Year Award for 2009. Just four and a half years later Sporting News ranked him the worst GM in baseball. Amaro jr. was fired 16 months later.

Al Hill – Flyers/C (1977-89) Al Hill spent his entire professional career with the Flyers organization and is currently a pro scout for the orange and black. Though he played three times as many games in the AHL as he did in the NHL, Hill is still in the NHL record books. On February 14th, 1977 Hill scored 2 goals and assisted on 3 others to record an NHL record 5 points in his NHL debut. Hill was called up to the big club earlier in the day. A snowstorm nearly kept Hill from making the game. He started the game on Bobby Clarke's line and scored his first NHL goal just 36 seconds in. The goal was assisted by future Hall of Famer Bobby Clarke and future Flyer Head Coach Terry Murray. Hill turned his NHL record night into his first Gordie Howe hat trick when he dropped the gloves against St. Louis Blues leading scorer Bob McMillan. The Flyers defeated the Blues 6-4. Hill would only earn one more assist at the NHL level that season.

Did you know...

... Fyers captain Eric Desjardins is the only NHL defenseman to score a hat trick in the Stanley Cup Finals (June 3rd, 1993 w/Montreal Canadiens).

... Phillies GM Ruben Amaro jr., once played his father in an episode of TV show The Goldbergs.

... On August 25th, 1995, Phillies pitcher Jeff Juden hit a grand slam setting an NL record as the 3rd NL pitcher to hit a GS that season.

... Ruben Amaro jr. and Ruben Amaro sr. are the only father-son combo in Phillies history. They both also played for the California Angels.

... Flyers Al Hill was the 1st Flyer to wear #37. He is also the first Flyers non-goalie to have the highest sweater number on the roster.

... Flyers Hall of Famer Bernie Parent once started a team-record 37 consecutive games in goal (October 11th, 1973 thru January 10th, 1974).

... Eagles RB Tom Woodeshick holds the team record for games played by a RB w/ 111.

Oddly enough...

37... The 1994-95 Sixers team had a team-record 37.9 3-point FG shooting pct.

37... Phillies Ryan Howard was intentionally walked a team-record 37 times in 2006.

38

Curt Schilling – Phillies/P (1992-2000) Curt Schilling was a hard-throwing power pitcher who was the Phillies ace for much of the 1990's. Schilling was the Phillies opening Day starter in five of his nine seasons with the team. He was part of the Phillies famed Macho Row and helped the Phillies to their fifth World Series appearance in 1993 and was named the NLCS MVP. During his time in Phillies pinstripes, Schilling was a three-time All Star, two-time NL strikeout leader, three-time NL complete game leader, and twice had 300+ strikeouts in a season. He won the Lou Gehrig Memorial Award in 1995. Schilling, not one to shy away from expressing his opinion, was known for his outspokenness and run-ins with teammates, management, media, and politicians. Schilling, who is 15th all-time with 3,116 strikeouts, is only one of two pitchers with 3000+ strikeouts not in the Hall of Fame (Roger Clemens). Though snubbed so far by Cooperstown, Schilling entered the Phillies Wall of Fame in 2012.

Larry Christenson – Phillies/P (1973-83) Larry Christenson was the Phillies number 1 draft pick in 1972 and played his entire MLB career with the Phillies. Christenson pitched a complete game 7-1 win over the New York Mets in his MLB debut. Christenson was the youngest player in the Majors for two and a half months. Christenson was an important part of the Phillies rotation that put the Phillies in the postseason 1976-78, won the World Series in 1980. Christenson had his best season in 1977 when he won 19 games. The Phillies won each of Christenson's final eight starts in 1977 leading up to the postseason. Christenson won seven of them. On August 29th, 1977 vs. Atlanta Braves, Christenson pitched nine innings and left the game with a 2-2 tie. The Phillies won the game in the 14th inning. The no-decision kept Christenson from being the Phillies first 20-game winner to come through their system since Chris Short in 1966. As of 2019, the Phillies are still waiting for their next home-grown 20 game winner.

Rick Wise – Phillies/P (1966-71) Rick Wise won his first MLB game 8-2 on June 21st, 1964 in the second game of a double header vs. New York Mets. In the 1st game of the twinbill, Jim Bunning pitched his historic perfect game. Wise almost had a perfect game of his own when he pitched a no-hitter for the Phillies on June 23rd, 1971 vs. Cincinnati Reds giving up just one walk. Wise hit two HRs in the game. On August 28th that same year vs. San Francisco Giants, Wise once again had a two-homer game. Wise was a 1971 NL All Star and retired 28 batters in a row later that season. The following season Wise was traded to the St. Louis Cardinals for Steve Carlton in one of the most lopsided trades in MLB history. Wise finished his career tied for 21st all-time in HRs by a pitcher with 15.

Did you know...

... The Phillies have been to the World Series 7 times in 136 years. Three of those appearances came within a 14-year period (1980, 1983, 1993).

... Phillies pitcher Curt Schilling appeared in the postseason with three teams (Philadelphia, Arizona, Boston). His .846 postseason winning percentage, (11-2 record) is MLB record (10+ postseason appearances).

... Phillies pitcher Curt Schilling has the highest strikeout to walk ratio of any pitcher in MLB history with 3000+ career KOs.

... Phillies pitcher Curt Schilling was born in Anchorage Alaska. In 136 years of Phillies baseball, he is the only Alaskan-born player to ever play for the team.

... Phillies pitcher Kyle Kendrick, while playing for the Phillies, married Stephenie LaGrossa, a three-time contestant on the reality TV show Survivor.

Even up...

38... The 2017 Eagles had a team-record 38 passing TDs. Carson Wentz had a team-record 33, and Nick Foles, who would lead them to a Super Bowl LII victory, had 5.

39

Brett Myers – Phillies/P (2002-09) Brett Myers was a starting pitcher turned reliever turned starter over his Phillies career. Myers was a part of the Phillies 2008 World Series Champions. In 2006, despite taking a leave of absence from the team after a domestic assault on his wife, Myers led the Phillies in wins, ERA, and strikeouts. Myers was the Phillies opening day starter in 2007 but moved to the bullpen after only 3 starts. Myers shined in the closer role finishing 2007 with 21 saves. Myers flashed his temper again in August during a confrontation with a member of the media. Myers was 3rd in the NL in strikeouts in 2005 with 208, and 5th in 2006 with 189. Myers had three errorless seasons for the Phils (2004, 2006, 2008).

Robbie Moore – Flyers/G (1978-79) Robbie Moore made his NHL debut with the Flyers on March 6th, 1979 after Hall of Famer Bernie Parent went down with a career-ending injury. Moore defeated the Colorado Rockies 5-0 becoming the 15th goalie in NHL history and the only Flyer to record a shutout in his NHL debut. Moore had two shutouts in the 5 games he played, finishing 9th in the NHL in shutouts though he only played five games. In the minors, Moore was one of the first goalies to handle the puck like a defenseman. As a Maine Mariner, Moore was a three-time winner of the Harry "Hap" Holmes Memorial Award given to the AHL team with the lowest goals against average. Moore won it in 1979 in tandem with Pete Peeters, in 1980 with Rick St. Croix, and in 1981 with Pelle

Lindbergh. At 5'5", Robbie Moore was the shortest goalie in Flyers history.

Did you know...

... Phillies pitcher Brett Myers once released a rock/country EP called Backwoods Rebel.

... As the Phillies opening day starter-turned closer, Brett Myers threw both the first and last pitches of the 2007 Phillies season.

Oddly enough...

39... Keeping up with the Joneses. There have been 39 Joneses on the big four sports teams (9-Phillies, 16-Eagles, 4-Flyers, 10-Sixers).

39... The 2017-18 season marked the 39th time the Flyers have made the postseason in their history.

39... Flyers defensemen Eric Desjardins and Mark Howe hold the team record for power play goals by a defenseman, each scoring 39 during their Flyers careers.

39... Sixers Wilt Chamberlain scored a team-record 39 1st half points in a 132-125 win over the LA Lakers on February 7th, 1966.

39... Sixers Hal Greer (2/14/59 vs Boston), Wilt Chamberlain (12/16/67 vs Chicago), and Allen Iverson (4/12/97 vs Cleveland) hold the Sixers team record for 2nd half points in a game with 39.

40

Tom Brookshier – Eagles/DB (1953, 1956-61) Tom Brookshier played his entire seven-season career for the Birds. Brookshier made his Eagles debut in 1953 but missed the 1954 and 1955 seasons while in the military. Brookshier was a two-time Pro Bowler and was a starter for the 1960 Eagles NFL Championship team. On November 5th, 1961 in a game against the Chicago Bears, Brookshier suffered a career-ending leg injury. Brookshier had a very successful second career in broadcasting both at the national and local level. Brookshier's #40 was retired and Brookie entered the Eagles Hall of Fame in 1989.

Steve Bedrosian – Phillies/P (1986-89) Steve Bedrosian was a starting pitcher in the NL for five seasons before coming to the Phillies and being moved to the bullpen. Bedrock had 29 saves for the Phillies in 1986, his first season with the team and first in the bullpen. Bedrosian had a career year in 1987 recording a league leading 40 saves, an NL All Star nod, the NL Rolaids Relief Man Award and the 1987 Cy Young Award.

John Denny – Phillies/P (1982-85) John Denny was brought in to solidify the Phillies rotation in 1982. He had the best season of his career in 1983, going 19-6 with a 2.37 ERA, helping the Wheeze Kids to the 1983 World Series vs. Baltimore Orioles and winning the 1983 Cy Young Award. Denny led all starting pitchers with 8 errors in 1983, but just two seasons later enjoyed an errorless 1985 posting a league-best 1.000 fielding pct.   The season before Denny joined the Phillies, he had the infamous on-field brawl with Yankee slugger Reggie Jackson on September 24th, 1981.

Did you know...

... Eagles great Tom Brookshier was born in Roswell, New Mexico.

... From 1977 to 1987, a span of eleven seasons, Phillies Pitchers won 5 Cy Young Awards; Steve Carlton (1977, 1980, 1982), John Denny (1983), and Steve Bedrosian (1987). During the team's other 125 seasons, they had just two; Steve Carlton (1972), and Roy Halladay (2010).

... Phillies pitcher John Denny won the 1983 Cy Young Award. He was the first Phillies right-hander in team history to win it.

... Phillies pitcher Andy Ashby went an unspectacular 1-5 for the Phils during his 1st season in the big leagues. However, Ashby did what no other Phillies pitcher had ever done before or since. On June 15th, 1991, Ashby threw an immaculate 4th inning (3 KOs on 9 pitches) in a 3-1 loss to the Cincinnati Reds. Then, on October 6th, 1991 Ashby had another 4th inning feat, this time getting 3 outs on 3 pitches in a 7-0 loss to the New York Mets. No other Phillies pitcher has had both an immaculate inning and a 3-pitch 3-out inning in a career, much less their 1st 8 big league starts. Ashby's immaculate inning came in just his second MLB game.

41

Chris Short – Phillies/P (1959-72) Chris Short was a dominant pitcher for the Phillies in the mid-to-late 1960s. The two-time NL All Star had 83 wins over a five-year period including 20 wins in 1966. Short is 4th all-time on the Phillies leaders list in wins (135), shutouts (24), innings pitched (2,253), and strikeouts (1,585). Short was part of the 1964 Phillies team that blew a 6 1/2 game lead with 12 games to go. Though Short and Hall of Famer Jim Bunning started 8 of the last 12 games, the two stars couldn't overcome poor hitting and awful fielding. Short, a native of Milford, DE, entered the Phillies Wall of Fame in 1992.

Keith Byars – Eagles/RB (1986-92) Keith Byars was an outstanding running back for the Eagles. Whether he was rushing the rock, catching it out of the backfield, or blocking for his teammates, Byars always gave it his all. Byars, during the 1990 season, even threw for four touchdowns (on four receptions). Byars was 3rd in the league with 81 receptions and was All Pro in 1990. Byars rushed for 2,672 yards with 17 TDs and had 3,532 yards receiving with 13 TDs. Byars' 6 TD passes (on 6 career completions) is 3rd most for a RB in NFL history. Byars was named to the Eagles 75th Anniversary team.

Randy Logan – Eagles/S (1973-83) Randy Logan played his entire 11-year career with the Birds and was a starter on the Eagles team that went to the Super Bowl in 1980. Logan was 2nd Team All NFL in 1980. Logan was a Vermeil favorite and still has the 2nd longest consecutive games played streak with 159 (Harold Carmichael). Logan's 23 career INTs is 10th on Eagles all-time list.

Did you know...

... On October 2nd, 1965, Chris Short struck out 18 batters in 15 shutout innings in a no-decision Vs New York Mets. The game ended 0-0 in 18 innings.

... In 1966 Chris Short won 20 games for the Phillies. No other Phillies pitcher that has come up through the Phillies system has been a 20-game winner since, 52 years and counting.

Oddly enough...

41... Flyers Hall of Famer Eric Lindros holds the team record for goals by a rookie scoring 41 in 1992-93.

41... In 2003 the Eagles had a team-record 41 1st downs off opponent's penalties.

41... On April 5th, 1967, Sixers legend Wilt Chamberlain had a team-record 41 rebounds in a playoff game vs Boston Celtics.

41... The Phillies lost 111 games during the 1941 season, the most in team history.

42

Robert Esche – Flyers/G (2002-07) Robert Chico Esche was an American-born goalie who played four season for the orange and black. Esche led the Flyers to the Eastern Conference Finals in 2004. Esche won the William M Jennings Trophy with Roman Cechmanek (tied with Brodeur) in 2003.   Chico won the Yanick Dupre Class Guy Award in 2003, the Pelle Lindbergh Memorial Award in 2004, and was the starting goalie for Team USA at the World Cup of Hockey. Esche was also a member of the 2006 Team USA Men's Olympic Hockey Team at the 2006 Turin Olympics.

Jerry Stackhouse – Sixers/G-F (1995-98) Jerry Stackhouse was hyped to be the next Michael Jordan coming out of North Carolina. Though he may not have turned out to rival Jordan's accomplishments, he did play 18 years in the league and was the 106th NBA player in league history to score 15,000 points. Stackhouse burst on the scene with the Sixers in 1995 and led the team in scoring with 19.2 points per game average. He was named NBA 1st Team All-Rookie for the 1995-96 season. Stackhouse was dealt to the Detroit Pistons in December of 1997 in a trade that brought Simon Gratz HS and Temple University star, Aaron McKie to the team.

Ron Reed – Phillies/P (1976-83) Ron Reed was a solid relief pitcher for the Phillies for eight seasons. He was a member of the Phillies 1980 World Series Championship team and the 1983 Phillies World Series losing team. He led the MLB with 13 relief wins in 1979. Reed pitched in the very first NLCS with Atlanta (vs. New York Mets) in 1969, and the very first NLDS in 1981 with the Phillies (vs. Montreal Expos). Reed also pitched in five NLCS with the Phillies (1976 vs Reds, 1977 vs Dodgers, 1978 vs. Dodgers, 1980 vs. Astros, and 1983 vs. Dodgers). Reed is in a very elite club with 100+ wins, 100+ saves, and 50+ complete games. He is one of only five pitchers to ever accomplish this.

Chris Maragos – Eagles/S (2014-2018) Chris Maragos was the Birds special teams captain. On December 6th, 2015 Maragos blocked a punt that Najee Goode returned for a touchdown in a 35-28 win over the New England Patriots. Maragos went down with a knee injury in week six of the 2017 season and watched his teammates go on to win Super Bowl LII.

Did you know...

... Ron Reed was the winning pitcher for the Atlanta Braves on April 8th 1974, the night Hank Aaron hit his record-breaking 715th home run.

... Phillies pitcher Ron Reed was drafted 3rd overall in the 1965 NBA Draft by the Detroit Pistons. He played 119 games with the NBA Pistons before turning to baseball.

... On January 19th, 2002, Eagles back-up safety Rashard Cook had a sack and an INT vs Chicago Bears in a 33-19 Eagles win in the 2001 Conference Semi Final. He's the only Eagle to ever have a sack and an INT in the same playoff game.

... Sixers Elton Brand was a founding member of Gibraltar Films, a movie production company. Their 1st film release was Rescue Dawn starring Christian Bale in 2006.

Even up...

42... Flyers tough guy Dave "the hammer" Schultz had an NHL Record 42 PIMs in a playoff game on April 22nd, 1976 vs. Toronto Maple Leafs.

42... Flyers consecutive home victories over the Pittsburgh Penguins from February 7th, 1974 to December 8th, 1988.

42... On October 1st, 1955 the Eagles and Washington Redskins combined for 42 3rd-quarter points. Washington scored 28, the Eagles had 14. The six total 3rd-quarter TDs is an Eagles team record.

42... On December 7th, 1947 the Eagles and the Chicago Cardinals combined for 42 4th-quarter points. Chicago scored 28, the Eagles had 14. The six total 4th-quarter TDs is an Eagles team record.

43

Randy Wolf – Phillies/P (1999 -2006) Randy Wolf pitched 8 seasons for the Phillies and was a 2003 NL All Star. Wolf, a pretty good-hitting pitcher hit two homers for the Phillies on August 11th, 2004 vs Colordo Rockies. Wolf's 7.43 strikeouts per 9 innings ranks 6th best in team history, and his 971 strikeouts ranks 10th. Wolf had his own fan club called the Wolf Pack who hung out in the centerfield upper deck at Vet Stadium and howled for every Wolf strikeout.

Darren Sproles – Eagles/RB-PR (2014-present) Darren Sproles was a member of the Eagles 2017 season Super Bowl LII Champs. The three-time Eagles Pro Bowler was 2nd team All-Pro in 2014. Sproles had a 49-yard TD run in his Eagles debut, the longest rush from scrimmage in his career. Sproles led the NFL with 506 punt return yards in 2014. It was the 2nd highest single-season punt return yardage in Eagles team history. Sproles was a three-time NFC Special Teams Player of the Week and once an NFC Offensive Player of the Week. Sproles had an NFL-record 2,696 all-purpose yards for the New Orleans Saints in 2011. Sproles sits 8th on the NFL's career all-purpose yards list with 19,164. At the close of the 2017 NFL season, Sproles had the most career all-purpose yards than any other active NFL player. Sproles is tied with DeSean Jackson for most career punt return TDs in Eagles history with 4. On September 25th, 2017, Sproles broke his arm and tore his ACL on the same play, ending his season during the Eagles run to their first-ever Super Bowl Championship.

Roynell Young – Eagles/DB (1980-88) Roynell Young played his entire eight-year NFL career with the Eagles. Young was a rookie on the 1980 Eagles team that appeared in Super Bowl XV vs Oakland Raiders. Young was an NFL All-Rookie in 1980 and a 1981 Pro Bowler. Young was 8th in the NFL in INTs in 1982. Young is tied for 10th all-time on Eagles INT list with 23 career interceptions.

Martin Biron – Flyers/G (2007-09) Marty Biron was a very popular Flyer during his short stint with the team. Biron led the Flyers to the Eastern Conference Finals during the 2007-08 season, his first full season with the team. Biron became the 7th different goalie in Flyers history to hit 30+ wins in a season in 2007-08 compiling a 2.59 GAA and a .918 save pct.   Biron's career save pct with the Flyers at .915 is 3rd best in team history. His career team GAA of 2.71 is 10th best. On December 26th, 1995 Biron received a late Christmas gift in the form of his first NHL call-up and subsequent NHL start for the Buffalo Sabres, becoming at the time the 4th youngest goalie to make his NHL debut start.

Did you know...

... Flyer defenseman Andy Delmore tied an NHL record for goals scored in a playoff game by a defenseman when he scored a hat trick against the Pittsburgh Penguins in a 6-3 Flyers win. The win put them up 3 games to 2 on May 7th, 2000. It was three days after the Flyers record-breaking 5 overtime victory.

... Phillies pitcher Randy Wolf purchased a home in the Hollywood Hills from Slash of Guns 'N Roses.

... Eagles Roynell Young and Ron Baker are the only two players that appeared in both Super Bowl XV (January 25th, 1981 vs. Oakland Raiders) and the Fog Bowl (December 31st, 1988 vs Chicago Bears).

Oddly enough...

43... Flyers Ron Hextall had an NHL Record 43 PIMs by a goaltender in a single playoff year in 1986-87.

43... In 1943, Phillies owner Robert Carpenter tried unsuccessfully to change the Phillies name to the Blue Jays.

43... Sixer Wilt Chamberlain had a team-record 43 rebounds in a 103-98 victory over the Boston Celtics on March 6th, 1965.

44

Kimmo Timonen – Flyers/D (2007-14) Kimmo Timonen came to the Flyers in a trade that also brought Scott Hartnell. Immediately following the trade, Timonen signed a six-year deal with the Flyers that made him the highest paid Finnish player in NHL history. Timonen was a three-time All Star and a five-time Barry Ashbee Trophy winner. Timonen, a future Flyer Hall of Famer played in five consecutive Olympics with Team Finland (1998, '02, '06, '10, '14) winning one silver medal and three bronze.

Pete Retzlaff – Eagles/TE (1956-66 player, 1969-72 VP and GM) Pistol Pete Retzlaff played his entire 11-yr career with the Eagles. Retzlaff was a member of the Eagles 1960 NFL Championship team. The five-time Pro Bowler was twice a 1st Team All Pro, and twice a 2nd team All Pro. Retzlaff was a RB in college. In his third year as a pro, Retzlaff led the NFL with 56 receptions. Retzlaff won the Bert Bell Award in 1965. Retzlaff served as the Eagles Vice President and GM from 1969-72. He entered the Eagles Hall of Fame in 1989 and had his #44 retired by the Birds.

Dick Ruthven – Phillies/P (1973-75, 1978-83) Dick Ruthven had two stints in Phillies pinstripes. Ruthven was the winning pitcher in relief in game 5 of the 1980 NLCS on their way to a World Series win. Ruthven was 5th in NL in wins with 17 in 1980, and was an NL All Star in 1981.

Did you know...

... Phillies pitcher Roy Oswalt once played an inning in leftfield for the Phillies when Ryan Howard was ejected from a game on August, 24th 2010. Oswalt played left field in the top of the 16th inning of a game against his former team the Houston Astros after Raul Ibanez moved to first to replace Howard. Oswalt recorded one putout during his inning in the outfield.

... Flyers defenseman Janne Niinimaa holds the team record for assists by a rookie defenseman notching 44 during in 1996-97.

... Flyers prospect Jussi Timonen, Kimmo Timonen's younger brother, played 14 games for the Flyers during the 2006-07 season, the season before Kimmo joined the team. Though they were both part of the Flyers organization for a time, they never played an NHL game together.

... On August 12th, 2016, Phillies P Jake Thompson did something no Phillies pitcher had ever done. During a game vs Colorado Rockies, Thompson recorded 4 strikeouts in the 2nd inning. Rockies David Dahl struck out on a wild pitch and reached 1st base safely. Gerardo Parra singled to right (Dahl to third), Nick Hundley reached base on an error (Dahl scored, Parra to 2B), Ben Paulsen, Daniel Descalso, and Jon Gray struck out to end the inning. To recap... 1 wild pitch, 1 error, 1 base hit, 1 run scored, 4 strikeouts. It was just Thompson's 2nd MLB game, and 6th MLB inning pitched. The 4K inning was the 81st in MLB modern era, and the 47th in the NL.

45

Tug McGraw – Phillies/P (1975-84) Tug McGraw will always be remembered for striking out Kansas City Royals outfielder Willie Wilson in game 6 of the 1980 World Series giving the Phillies their first-ever Championship. Tugger was an NL All Star in 1975. He is 1st in team history with 313 games finished. McGraw is 4th in games played (463), 6th in saves (94), and 6th fewest hits per 9 innings (7.891). In 2004 the Philadelphia Chapter of the Baseball Writers Association created the Tug McGraw Good Guy Award. Tugger entered the Phillies Wall of Fame in 1999, and was one of only two left-handed pitchers on the Phillies 1983 Centennial Team (Steve Carlton). Tugger passed away in 2004.

Terry Mulholland – Phillies/P (1989-93, 1996) Terry Mulholland pitched for six seasons for the Phillies. Mulholland was known for his deadly pick-off move and his ability to consistently throw strikes. On August 15th, 1990 Mulholland no-hit his former team, the San Francisco Giants at Veterans Stadium, winning 6-0. It was the 1st no-hitter ever at the Vet. It was also the 1st no-hitter by a pitcher against his former team in 26 years. Mulholland was the starting NL pitcher for the 1993 All Star game, the first Phillies pitcher so-honored in 14 years (Steve Carlton) and only the second in 38 years (Robin Roberts). Mulholland was the starting pitcher in game six of the 1993 World Series, the fateful game where Mitch Williams gave up a walk-off series-clinching homer to Toronto Blue Jay Joe Carter.

Tim Hauck – Eagles/S (1999-01 player, 2016-present coach) Tim Hauck spent three seasons with the Birds and was an outstanding special teamer. Hauck is most remembered for the crushing hit he put on Dallas Cowboy receiver Michael Irvin in 1999. Irvin suffered a spinal injury that ended his career. Hauck has been the Eagles safeties coach for the past two seasons and was part of the Eagles Super Bowl LII champion coaching staff.

Did you know...

... Phillies Tug McGraw was the last of Casey Stengel's players to play in the league.

... In 1999, Phillies Tug McGraw was in an episode of Everybody Loves Raymond.

... Terry Mulholland's MLB career lasted 5 days short of 20 years. During his career, Mulholland beat every single team in Major League Baseball.

... Terry Mulholland, as a member of the San Francisco Giants, once fielded a sharply hit ball that got stuck in his glove webbing. He threw the runner out by throwing his glove to first base.

... 2015 Hall of Fame inductee Pedro Martinez became just the 10th pitcher in MLB history to reach 100 wins in both leagues when he notched his third win in a Phillie uniform on September 3rd, 2009.

Oddly enough...

45... Johnson & Johnson and more Johnsons... There have been 45 Johnsons on the big four sports teams, the Flyers' Kim Johnsson notwithstanding... (11-Phillies, 27-Eagles, 1-Flyer, 6-Sixers).

45... Flyers Hall of Famer Mark Howe holds the team record for postseason assists by a defenseman with 45 playoff assists during his Flyers career.

45... Flyers Ron Hextall holds the team record for playoff wins notching 45 during his Flyers career, including 15 in his Conn Smythe-winning 1987 playoff performance.

45... Eagles Super Bowl XXXIX QB Donovan McNabb was the 45th QB in team history to start a game for the Eagles.

45... On November 15th, 2010 the Eagles scored a team-record 45 1st-half points on their way to a 59-28 win over the Washington Redskins. The combined score of 87 points for the game tied a team record.

45... Phillies reliever Jose Mesa had a team-record 45 saves during the 2002 season.

46

Herm Edwards – Eagles/DB (1977-85) Herm Edwards will always and forever be remembered for recovering a Joe Pisarcik fumble for a 26-yard touchdown in the closing moments of a November 19th, 1978 game against the New York Giants, known as the Miracle of the Meadowlands. The fumble recovery changed the fortunes for both teams that season. Two years later Edwards was a member of the Eagles Super Bowl XV team that lost to the Oakland Raiders. Edwards career 33 INTs is second most in franchise history. Edwards played 135 consecutive games for the Eagles, never missing a single game during his Eagle's tenure.

Jon Dorenbos – Eagles/LS (2006-2017) Jon Dorenbos was a long-snapper for the Eagles. The two-time Pro Bowler played 162 consecutive games for the Eagles. His 162 games played is 6th most in Eagles history. A trade to the New Orleans Saints and subsequent physical revealed a congenital aortic aneurysm. Dorenbos underwent a 10-hour life-saving surgery. Dorenbos joined his former team for their Super Bowl parade and received an honorary Super Bowl Ring from the Eagles.

Ryan Madson – Phillies/P (2003-11) Ryan Madson was a member of the Phillies 2008 World Series Championship team. Madson was an outstanding set-up man during the team's World Series run and was the "Bridge to Lidge" (Phillies closer Brad Lidge). Madson took over the closer role for the Phils in 2011 and had a career high 32 saves. Madson closed out his Phillies career with a 47-30 record with 52 saves.

Kevin Gross – Phillies/P (1983-88) Kevin Gross pitched six seasons for the Phillies. He is 14th on Phillies all-time strikeout leader list, 24th in games started, and 34th in wins. Gross was one of two Phillies named to the 1988 NL All Star team, along with his battery mate Lance Parrish.

Did you know...

... Eagles long snapper Jon Dorenbos was born in Humble, Texas.

... Eagles long snapper Jon Dorenbos is a very talented magician. He finished 3rd on season 11 of America's Got Talent.

... Phillies pitcher Ryan Madson's uncle, Steve Barr, played in the American League in the mid-1970's.

... On August 10th, 1987, Phillies pitcher Kevin Gross was caught with sandpaper in his glove and was subsequently suspended for 10 games.

Even up...

46... There have been 46 Smiths on the big four sports teams, the Flyers Greg Smyth notwithstanding... (11-Phillies, 28-Eagles, 3-Flyers, 4-Sixers).

47

Larry Andersen – Phillies/P (1983-86, 1993-94) Larry Andersen played six of his nineteen MLB seasons with the Phillies. Andersen, known for a killer slider and huge personality sits 26th on Phillies games played list (241), and 29th in games finished (73). L.A. has been a part of the Phillies broadcast team since 1998.

Did you know...

... Phillies pitcher turned broadcaster Larry Anderson appeared in both the 1983 and 1993 World Series for the Phillies. He is the only Phillies player to do so.

Oddly enough...

47... Flyers Hall of Fame goalie Bernie Parent holds the NHL record for regulation-time wins by a goalie in one season with 47 wins during their 1st Stanley Cup season 1973-74.

47... The Flyers won 47 games in back-to-back seasons in 2010-11 and 2011-12.

48

Wes Hopkins – Eagles/S (1983-93) Wes Hopkins played his entire 11-year NFL career with the Eagles.   Hopkins was a Pro bowler, 1st team All Pro, and Eagles team defensive MVP in 1985. He was also NFC defensive player of the week for week three of the 1985 season. Hopkins had three seasons in the top ten in INTs. His 30 career INTs is 5th all-time on the Eagles list. Hopkins teamed with Andre Waters to create one of the fiercest safety tandems in the league as part of the Eagles legendary Gang Green defense. Hopkins was awarded the Ed Block Courage Award in 1988.

Danny Briere – Flyers/C (2008-13) Danny Briere was a skilled big-game fan favorite for the Flyers. During the 2010 Stanley Cup playoffs, Briere led all scorers with 30 points (12g 18a) breaking Flyers team record held by Brian Propp (28). Briere's 12 points in the Finals alone was one point shy of Wayne Gretzky's record. Briere elevated his game when the playoffs arrived. He notched 37 goals and 72 points in 68 playoff games for the orange and black. Briere was a 2011 NHL All Star for the Flyers. Briere is currently running the Comcast Spectacor-owned Maine Mariners of the ECHL that begins play in 2018-19.

Even up...

48... The Sixers have been to the postseason 48 times in team history.

48... On February 12th, 1961 the Sixers (Nationals) scored a team-record 48 2nd quarter points in a 148-122 victory over the Detroit Pistons.

48... Only 9 players have worn the #48 in Eagles team history. FB Jon Ritchie (WIP radio host) was the most recent. It's the fewest number of players for any non-kicker, non-QB, non-retired number on the team.

49

Jose Mesa – Phillies/P (2001-03, 2007)   Jose Mesa only pitched four seasons for the Phillies, but his 112 career saves as a phillie is 2nd best in team history. Mesa had back-to-back 40+ save seasons. Mesa also ranks 23rd on the Phillies all-time list in games played (246) and 9th in games finished (183). In Mesa's second stint with the Phillies in 2007, he tasted Phillies postseason baseball for the first time. But the taste was sour. Mesa Phinished his Phillies career (and his MLB career) by giving up two walks and three earned runs in a third of an inning for a 81.00 era in a game two 10-5 defeat to the Colorado Rockies.

Tommy Greene – Phillies/P (1990-95) Tommy Greene was a hard-throwing pitcher that came to the Phillies in the Dale Murphy trade. On May 23rd, 1991, Greene threw the 8th no-hitter in Phillies history, a 2-0 win over the Montreal Expos. It was just his 15th MLB start. Greene finished 1993 tied with teammate Curt Schilling with a team-leading 16 wins. Greene finished 6th in Cy Young voting that season. Greene started game 4 of the 1993 World Series vs. Toronto Blue Jays. He left the game with a 6-5 lead in a no-decision as the Phillies lost 15-14. Greene's career was cut short by chronic shoulder issues.

Did you know...

... Flyers Brian Savage (2005-06) is the nephew of Flyers brother duo Wayne and Larry Hillman.

... Phillies pitcher Vance "the Vanimal" Worley finished 3rd in Rookie of the Year voting in 2011 after going 11-3 with a 3.01 ERA, and having one of the greatest nicknames ever.

Oddly enough...

49... Flyers defenseman Behn Wilson holds the team record for points by a rookie defenseman, notching 49 points during the 1978-79 season.

50

Jamie Moyer – Phillies/P (2006-10) Sellersville, PA native Jamie Moyer is the oldest MLB pitcher to win a game and oldest player to record an RBI in MLB history. Moyer played 25 seasons in the bigs, appearing in games spanning four decades (80's, 90's, 00's, 10's) and is only the 8th MLB pitcher to accomplish this. On April 13, 2007 Moyer struck out his 2000th batter in a game vs. Atlanta Braves with Tom Glavine as the Braves starter. It was the oldest combined age for lefty vs lefty in league history at the time, with a combine age of 85. Three months later, Moyer faced off against David Wells, setting a new record for lefty starters combined age with 88 years. In 2008, at 45 years old, Moyer started his first World Series game as the Phillies faced off against the Tampa Bay Rays. Moyer won 56 games with the Phillies over 5 seasons.

Guy Morriss – Eagles/C (1973-83) Guy Moriss did a lot of hiking during his 11 seasons as an Eagle. Moriss, however, didn't cover a ton of ground. He spent his time in the trenches. The stalwart Eagles center is 9th all-time on the Eagles games played list with 158. Moriss was the Eagles starting center for their Super Bowl XV team vs. Oakland Raiders.

Steve Mix – Sixers/F (1973-82) Steve "the Mayor" Mix played 9 seasons with the Sixers. The 1975 NBA All Star made it to the NBA finals 3 times with the Sixers (1977, 80, and 82). Mix is 8th on the Sixers all-time list for games played (668), 8th in defensive rebounds (2,453), 5th in offensive rebounds (1,318), and 6th in steals (851). Mix was part of the Sixers broadcast team for 22 years.

Garry Cobb – Eagles/LB (1985-87) Garry Cobb was an Eagles linebacker and part of Buddy Ryan's vaunted Gang Green defense. Cobb was defensive player of the week for week #5 of the 1986 season when he recorded a team record 4 sacks (since broken), a forced fumble, and fumble recovery in a 16-0 win over the Atlanta Falcons. Cobb runs GCobb.com, covering all things Eagles.

Did you know...

... Phillies P Jamie Moyer, upon retiring, had faced 8.9% of all MLB hitters to ever play the game.

... Phillies Jamie Moyer made his MLB debut with the Chicago Cubs on June 16th, 1986, beating Steve Carlton and his hometown Phillies to earn his 1st big league win.

Even up...

50... On September 3rd, 2006, Ryan Howard became first Phillie in team history to hit 50 home runs in a single season. Howard finished the 2006 season with a career high 58 HRs.

50... On April 3rd 1980, Flyers sniper Reggie Leach became the only Flyer to score his 50th goal of a season into an open net, doing so vs. Washington Capitals.

50... The Flyers have had six different players hit the 50-goal mark in their history (Rick MacLeish, Reg Leach, Bill Barber, Mark Recchi, Tim Kerr, and John LeClair).

50... Flyers legendary goalie Bernie Parent had 50 career shutouts with the Flyers, most in team history.

50... Phillies Jamie Moyer pitched in 50 MLB stadiums during his 25 MLB seasons.

50... On November 17th, 2013, Eagles punter Donnie Jones had a team-record net punt average of 50.7 yards per punt vs Washington Redskins.

50... Eagles WR/PR DeSean Jackson holds the Eagles team rookie-record for punt returns in a season with 50 in 2008.

50... On December 16th, 1962, the Sixers (Nationals) scored a team-record 50 1st quarter points against the San Francisco Warriors in a 144-137 win.

51

Carlos Ruiz – Phillies/C (2006-16) Carlos Ruiz was a mainstay behind the plate for the Phillies for a decade. Chooch had a penchant for delivering clutch hits in bigtime post-season spots earning him the nickname Senor Octubre. Ruiz was named to the TOPPS All Rookie Team for 2007. In game 3 of the 2008 World Series, Chooch had a World Series game-winning walk-off infield single, the first ever in World Series history. Ruiz caught the final out of the Phillies World Series clinching game over the Tampa Bay Rays. Chooch seemed to get better as he got older. He was a 2012 NL All Star, and garnered MVP votes three consecutive seasons (2010-2012). Ruiz caught an NL record-breaking four no-hitters as a Phillie. He caught Roy Halladay's perfect game and his no-hitter in 2010. It was the first time in 38 years that a catcher caught two no-hitters in the same season. He then caught the Phillies combined no-hitter in 2014 (Hamels, Diekman, Giles, Papelbon) and Cole Hamels no-hitter in Hamels' final game as a Phillie in 2015. Ruiz won the Major League Baseball Players Alumni Association Heart and Hustle Award for 2012.

Reggie Wilkes – Eagles/LB (1978-85) Reggie Wilkes was a linebacker during the Eagles run to Super Bowl XV vs Oakland Raiders. As a rookie for the Eagles in 1978, Wilkes was tied with All Pro Bill Bergey for the team lead in fumble recoveries with 5. Wilkes is 20th all-time for defensive fumble recoveries for the Eagles (10).

William Thomas – Eagles/LB (1991-99) William Thomas came into the league in 1991 and found himself surrounded by greatness. Thomas started 7 games for the Birds and their world-beater defense Gang Green. Thomas was a Pro Bowler in 1995 and 1996. He had 33 sacks during his Eagle career and 18 INTs. Thomas did not miss a game during his first 6 seasons for the Birds. Thomas is a member of the 20/20 club with 37 career sacks and 27 career INTs.

Did you know…

… On June 26th, 2007 Ruiz, who would only rack up 24 steals in 1,069 games with the Phillies, stole home as part of a double steal vs. Cincinnati Reds in an 11-5 win.

… Eagles linebacker Carlos Emmons was the Eagles Team Defensive MVP in 2003.

Oddly enough…

51… Flyers Pelle Eklund holds the team record for assists for a rookie, notching 51 during the 1985-86 season.

51… The Eagles scored just 51 points the entire 12-game season in 1936. They won their 1st game 10-7 over the New York Giants, and lost their last 11. They scored in double digits just twice and were shut out 6 times.

51… On March 2nd, 1963, the Sixers scored a team-record 51 3rd quarter points vs Detroit Pistons in a 152-128 victory.

52

Ricky Bottalico – Phillies/P (1994-98, 2001-02) Ricky Bottalico was a hard-throwing relief pitcher who spent two stints with the Phillies. In 1996, Bottalico was the Phillies' lone home team representative to the All Star Game that was played at Veterans Stadium that year. On August 2nd, 1998, in a game vs San Francisco Giants, Bottalico plunked Barry Bonds with a pitch. Bonds stormed after Bottalico and a bench-clearing brawl ensued. Bottalico spent seven seasons with the Phils, and ranks 8th on their all-time saves list with 78.

Did you know...

... Phillies reliever Ricky Bottalico was on an episode of the TV show Arli$$ in 1996.

Even up...

52... On February 4th, 2018 The Eagles defeated the New England Patriots 41-33 to win Super Bowl LII, their first Super Bowl Championship in team history.

52... Eagles Super Bowl LII MVP QB Nick Foles won Super Bowl 52 and was the 52nd QB to start a game for the Eagles in team history.

52... Eagles KR Quintin Demps holds the Eagles team rookie-record with 52 kickoff returns in 2008.

52... # of seasons (as of 2018) since the Phillies farm system produced a 20-game winning pitcher for the team (Chris Short 1966).

53

Hugh Douglas – Eagles/DE (1998-02, 2004) Hugh Douglas wreaked havoc on opposing quarterbacks during his two stints with the Birds. He was on the Eagles Super Bowl XXXIX team that lost to the Patriots. On October 18th, 1998, during his first season with the Eagles, Douglas had 4.5 sacks against the San Diego Chargers, tying the Eagles record. Douglas had 54.5 sacks for the Eagles during his 6 years with the team, good for 4th best on the Eagles' all-time list. Douglas had 184 tackles as an Eagle (34th best), and 6 forced fumbles (21st best) during his Eagles career. The outspoken Douglas once had an altercation with teammate Terrell Owens.

Bobby Abreau – Phillies/OF (1998-06) Bobby Abeau was one of the best hitters in team history. Abreau played 1,353 games for Phillies and is in the team's all-time top ten in doubles, on-base pct, slugging pct, runs, total bases, base on balls, and stolen bases. Abreau was a two-time NL All Star, three-time Phillies Player of the Year, a Silver Slugger Award winner in 2004 and a Gold Glove winner in 2005. Abreau led the NL in triples in 1999, doubles in 2002, and BBs in 2006.

Shayne Gostisbehere – Flyers/D (2014-present) On April 12th, 2014, Shayne Gostisbehere's college team, the Union Dutchmen, won the NCAA national championship defeating the Minnesota Golden Gophers, 7-4 at the Wells Fargo Center in Philly. Ghost was a +7 with 3 points. Three days later, Ghost signed his entry-level contract with the Flyers. On February 20, 2016 Ghost became the first rookie defenseman in NHL history to score his fourth overtime game-winning goal in a single season. He also tore off a 15-game point streak. Ghost was named to the 2015-16 NHL All Rookie Team, but was robbed in the Calder Trophy voting, finishing 2nd to Chicago Black Hawks Artemi Panarin. Ghost Bear was named the Gene Hart Memorial Award winner for 2015-16, and the Barry Ashbee Award winner for 2015-16, and 2017-18. Gostisbehere is the only Florida-born player to ever wear the orange and black.

Nigel Bradham – Eagles/LB (2016 – present) Nigel Bradham is a physical linebacker for the Eagles, helping the team to their Super Bowl LII Championship. Bradham had 186 total tackles for the Birds in two seasons, along with 3 sacks and a fumble recovery for a touchdown. Bradham signed a five-year deal with the Eagles in March 2018.

Ken Giles – Phillies/P (2014-15) Flamethrower Ken Giles and his 100 mph fastball rose quickly up the minor league ranks, making his Phillies debut on June 12th, 2014. Giles gave up a homer to Yasmani Grandal, the first batter he faced in his MLB debut. But there were bright spots during Giles' time with the Phils. On September 1st, 2014, Giles was part of the Phillies combined no-hitter, when he, Cole Hamels, Jake Diekman, and Jonathan Papelbon combined to no-hit the Atlanta Braves in a 7-0 Phillies win. Giles was 4th in NL Rookie of the Year voting for 2014.

Darryl Dawkins – Sixers/C (1975-82) Darryl Dawkins was a massive mass of humanity on the court. "Chocolate Thunder" obliterated two glass backboards with thunderous dunks in 1979 which prompted the NBA to adopt breakaway rims. Dawkins went to the NBA Finals three times as a Sixer but was traded away before the 1983 championship season. Along with Dawkins' penchant for thunderous dunks, and naming said dunks, Dawkins also had a penchant for fouling the opponent. During the 1982-83 season, Dawkins was called for an NBA record 379 personal fouls. He followed that up in 1983-84 by breaking his own NBA record with 386. Chocolate Thunder was the first player ever to join the NBA right out of high school.

Did you know...

... Phillies OF Bobby Abreau won the Home Run Derby at the 2005 MLB All Star game hitting 41 dingers.

... Bobby Abreau was the 1st Phillies player ever to join the 30-30 Club (30 HRs-30 SBs). Abreau not only did it in 2001, but did it again in 2004.

... According to former Sixer Darryl Dawkins, legendary recording artist Stevie Wonder nicknamed Dawkins "Chocolate Thunder!"

Oddly enough...

53... Flyers legends Rick MacLeish and Bill Barber hold the team record for most career playoff goals with 53.

53... Flyers Hall of Famer Mark Howe holds the team record for career playoff points by a defenseman with 53.

53... The Flyers set a team record for wins in a season, winning 53 in both the 1984-85 and 1985-86 seasons.

53... The Eagles scored 53 TDs in 2017 on their way to their 1st Super Bowl Championship. It's the 2nd most in team history.

53... On December 20th, 1967, the Sixers scored a team-record 53 4th quarter points vs Seattle Supersonics in a 160-122 victory. Their 95 total 2nd half points was also a team record.

54

Brad Lidge – Phillies/P (2008-11) Brad Lidge became a Philly Sports Immortal when he struck out Tampa Bay Rays' Eric Hinske in game 5 of the 2008 World Series to give the Phillies their 2nd championship, and Philadelphia its first major sports championship since 1983. Lidge was "lights out" during the 2008 season. He converted 41 of 41 save opportunities, the first Phillies' pitcher to have a perfect save pct season. He converted another 7 for 7 in the postseason. Lidge was named NL Rolaids Relief Man of the Year, DHL Delivery Man of the Year, and NL Comeback Player of the Year for 2008. He was also an NL All Star, finished 8th in MVP voting and 4th in Cy Young voting for 2008. 2009 was a very different story for "lights out". His save total dropped from 41 to 31 and his ERA ballooned from 1.95 to 7.21, the worst in MLB history among pitchers with at least 20 saves. Lidge officially retired as a Phillie.

Jeremiah Trotter – Eagles/LB (1998-01, 2004-06, 2009) Jeremiah "Axe Man" Trotter had three stints with the Birds. He was a member of their Super Bowl XXXIX team and was a 1st Team All Pro. Trotter's two INT TDs is tied for 6th best in Eagles history. His 564 tackles in 8th best, 25 passes defended is 19th best, and 7 forced fumbles is 13th best in Eagles history. In 2005 Trotter joined Maxie Baughan, Chuck Bednarik, and Bill Bergey as the only Eagles linebackers to be named to four+ Pro Bowls. In 2016, he joined them in the Eagles Hall of Fame.

Lucious Jackson – Sixers/C-F (1964-72) Lucious Jackson played his entire 8 season career with the Sixers. Luke was named to the 1965 NBA All Rookie 1st Team, and the NBA All Star Team, in a season that started just 4 days after he won a gold medal with Team USA basketball at the 1964 Summer Olympics in Tokyo, Japan. Jackson won an NBA Championship with the Sixers in 1967.

Did you know...

... Alternative pop/rock all-girl band Luscious Jackson (1996 hit Naked Eye) took their name from Sixers great Lucious Jackson.

Even up...

54... Gabe Kapler became the 54th manager in Phillies history when the team announced his hiring for the 2018 season.

54... The Flyers won 54 games at Nassau Veterans Memorial Coliseum in Uniondale, New York.

54... Flyer goalie Antero Niitymaki made a team-record 54 saves in a 3-2 Flyers win over the Toronto Maple Leafs on January 5th, 2008.

54... Eagles kicker Cody Parkey was a perfect 54 for 54 in PATs in 2014. Both the number of attempts and the number of completions are team records.

54... Eagles Allen Rossum had a team-record 54 kick-off returns for the Birds in 1999.

54... Eagles Wally Henry had a team-record 54 punt returns for the Birds in 1981.

54... The Eagles scored a team-record 54 TDs in 2014.

55

Dikembe Mutombo – Sixers/C (2001-02) Dikembe Mutombo played little more than a season in Philadelphia, but he was extremely popular with the Philly Faithful, and the Sixers do not go to the 2001 NBA Finals without him on the team. Mutombo was a defensive powerhouse and prolific shot blocker. Mutombo's humanitarian work, like his shot blocking, is also prolific. Dikembe entered the Sixers Hall of Fame and the NBA Hall of Fame in 2015.

Brandon Graham – Eagles/DE (2010 – present) Brandon Graham was selected 13th overall by the Eagles in the 2010 NFL Draft. Pro Football Focus rated Graham as the ninth best player in the NFL in 2016. Graham's 15 forced fumbles is 5th best in Eagles history and none was larger than the one he had on February 4th 2018 vs. New England Patriots. Graham attained Eagle immortality when he strip sacked Tom Brady with 2:21 remaining in Super Bowl LII. The fumble was recovered by Derek Barnett and all but assured an Eagles victory. Graham is currently 7th on Eagles all-time sack list with 38.5. Graham was the team's Defensive MVP for 2017.

Frank LeMaster – Eagles/LB (1974-82) Frank LeMaster spent all 9 seasons of his NFL career with the Eagles. He was a member of the Eagles Super Bowl XV team. LeMaster's 129 games played as an Eagle is a team 26th best. His 2 career INT TDs is tied for team 6th best and his longest (89 yards vs. Washington Redskins to close out the 1975 season) was the longest INT return in the NFL that year. LeMaster was selected to the 1981 Pro Bowl.

Did you known...

... Republic of Congo-born Dikembe Mutombo's full name is Dikembe Mutombo Mpolondo Mukamba Jean-Jacques Wamutombo.

... Sixers greats Allen Iverson and Dikembe Mutombo both attended Georgetown University.

... Flyers defenseman Frank Bathe was assessed a team-record 55 minutes in penalties in a game on March, 11th, 1979 vs Los Angeles Kings in a 6-3 Flyers win.

Oddly enough...

55... QB Carson Wentz is the 55th QB is team history to start a game for the Eagles.

55... On April 20th, 2003, Allen Iverson had a team-record 55 points in a playoff game in a 107-103 victory over the New Orleans Hornets.

55... Phillies 2008 World Series-winning Manager Charlie Manual owns the best Managerial winning pct. in team history with a .551 (780 wins - 636 losses).

56

Jerry Robinson – Eagles/LB (1979-84) Jerry Robinson spent the first six seasons of his NFL career with the Eagles. Robinson was selected for the NFL All Rookie team in 1979. On November 16th, 1980 Robinson recovered a fumble for a TD in a 24-0 win over the Washington Redskins. Robinson was selected to the 1981 Pro Bowl.

Byron Evans – Eagles/LB (1987-94) Byron Evans played his entire eight-year NFL career with the Eagles. He was a member of their famous Gang Green defense of 1991. Byron Evans was a very good linebacker but never received the notoriety that some of his more-famous Gang Green teammates did. However, Evans had the 2nd most tackles of any linebacker in Eagles history, and third most overall! On November 25th, 1990 Evans had a pick-six vs. New York Giants in a 31-13 Eagles win. On January 3rd, 1994 vs San Francisco 49ers, Evans ran a fumble recovery in for a TD in a 37-34 Eagles victory. Evans had 12 defensive fumble recoveries, 5th best for Eagles all-time.

Joe Blanton – Phillies/P (2008-12) Blanton was a member of the Phillies 2008 World Championship team. Blanton won game 4 of the 2008 World Series vs Tampa Bay Rays, and became the first pitcher in 34 years (and 13th ever) to homer in a World Series game. During the 2008 season, over half of Blanton's 111 KOs were "looking", the highest pct in MLB that year. Blanton was ignominiously the fifth starter on the Phillies Phantastic Phour staff of 2011 (Halladay, Lee, Hamels, Oswalt).

Chris Long – Eagles/DE (2017-Present) Chris Long is a hard-nosed defensive lineman who was part of the Eagles Super Bowl LII Championship Team. Long had 28 tackles, 5 sacks, 4 forced fumbles, and 11 passes defended for the 2017 season. He added 5 tackles in the 2017 playoffs. Chris Long, son of NFL Hall of Famer and Villanova star Howie Long, donated his entire 2017 salary to benefit education. Chris Long was the NFL's Walter Payton Man of the Year Award winner for 2018.

Did you know...

... Eagles DE Chris Long and RB LeGarrette Blount are only the third and fourth NFL players ever to have played for two different Super Bowl winners in consecutive years. Both Long and Blount won Super Bowl LI with the New England Patriots before winning again in Super Bowl LII with the Eagles (Ken Norton Dal/SF 1993-94, Deion Sanders SF/Dal 1994-95).

... Phillies catcher Andy Seminick hit two HRs in the same inning of the 1949 MLB All Star Game.

... Phillies Whiz Kids catcher Andy Seminick passed away in 2004. He was the last surviving everyday player from the 1950 Pennant-winning Phillies.

57

Bill Cowher – Eagles/LB (1979, 1983-84) Bill Cowher was a Hall of Fame Super Bowl-winning Head Coach of the Pittsburgh Steelers. But prior to that, Cowher had two stints with the Eagles as a linebacker/special teamer. He credits his time as a bubble player for helping him appreciate the efforts of the bubble player while a head coach. During a game against the Chicago Bears in 1983, Cowher tackled Bears punt-returner Jeff Fisher, breaking his leg. Fisher claims it's that injury that drove him into coaching where the two men became fierce rivals. The year after Cowher left the Eagles, Fisher joined them as a coach under Buddy Ryan.

Did you know...

... No Flyer and no Sixer has ever worn #57.

Oddly enough...

57... MLB record number of years Phillies went between no-hitters (Johnny Lush 5/1/1906, Jim Bunning 6/21/64). The two quickest Phillies no-hitters were both courtesy of Roy Halladay. Halladay's May 29th, 2010 perfect game, followed by Doc's first-ever postseason start and first no-hitter at Citizens Bank Park, October 6th, 2010, was a span of just 130 days.

57... Phillies pitcher Jack Sanford won the 1957 Rookie of the Year Award going 19-8 with a 3.08 ERA and 188 KOs.

58

Trent Cole – Eagles/LB-DE (2005-14) Trent Cole spent 10 seasons with the Birds terrorizing opposing quarterbacks. The two-time Pro Bowler was also 2nd team All Pro in 2009. On December 17th, 2006 Cole nabbed the only INT of his Eagles career, a pick-six vs New York Giants. Cole is 9th on the Eagles' all-time tackles list with 436, 3rd in forced fumbles with 19, and second only to Hall of Famer Reggie White on the Eagles all-time sack list with 85.5.   Cole added 2.5 sacks and 34 tackles in 8 postseason games. Cole was named to the 2005 NFL All Rookie Team. On Christmas Day 2017, Trent Cole retired as an honorary Eagle.

Ike Reese – Eagles/LB (1998-04) Ike Reese spent seven years with the Birds and was a standout special-teamer. Reese was a member of the Eagle's NFC champion team in 2004 that played in Super Bowl XXXIX vs New England Patriots. Reese was a special teams selection for the 2004 Pro Bowl. Reese is 17th on Eagles all-time list with 7 forced fumbles. Ike has been a part of sports radio in Philly since 2008. VICTORY!!!

Jordan Hicks – Eagles/LB (2015-present) Jordan Hicks is a hard-hitting exciting young linebacker. On November 8th, 2015 vs. Dallas Cowboys Hicks had a 67-yard pick six. Hicks has played just 31 games for the Birds so far, but has registered 163 tackles, 7 interceptions, 1 forced fumble, and 5 fumble recoveries. During the 2017 season, Hicks ruptured his

Achilles tendon in week #7, and was sidelined for the rest of the season, watching his teammates go on to win Super Bowl LII.

Jonathan Papelbon – Phillies/P (2012-15) Jonathon Papelbon was a polarizing figure in Philly sports. From obscene gestures to confrontational comments, love/hate has always been part of the Papelbon story. His etiquette may have been questionable, but his talent was not. Papelbon was a two-time All Star with the Phillies, and was part of their 2014 combined no hitter on September 1st (Hamels, Giles, Diekman, Papelbon). Papelbon became MLB 26th member of the 300-save club on June 10, 2014 vs. San Diego Padres. Papelbon, though he only spent three and a half seasons in Philly, is the team's all-time save leader.

Did you know...

... Phillies pitcher Jonathan Papelbon is not only the Phillies all-time saves leader, but the Boston Red Sox all-time leader, as well.

... Eagles linebacker Jordan Hicks had his first NFL sack and subsequent first NFL forced fumble in his second career game when he sacked Dallas Cowboy QB Tony Romo, breaking Romo's collarbone on the play.

Even up...

58... Phillies slugger Ryan Howard hit a career high 58 Homers in 2006 shattering Mike Schmidt's team record 48.

58... The Flyers won 58 games at the legendary Montreal Forum.

59

Seth Joyner – Eagles/LB (1986-93) Crushing hitter Seth Joyner played 8 seasons with the Birds. He was named to the 1991 Pro Bowl, and was part of the Eagles legendary Gang Green defense. Joyner made the Pro Bowl again in 1993, and was a three-time All Pro. Joyner is 2nd in forced fumbles with 21, 2nd in tackles with 875, and the Birds all-time leader with 3 fumble recoveries for touchdowns. Joyner was Sports Illustrated Defensive Player of the Year in 1991 and was named to the Eagles 75th Anniversary Team. Joyner joined the Eagles Hall of Fame in 2018.

Did you know...

... On December 2nd, 1991 vs. Houston Oilers on Monday Night Football, Eagles linebacker Seth Joyner had a game for the ages. He had 8 solo tackles, 2 sacks, 2 forced fumbles and 2 fumble recoveries. He also had a 102-degree temperature.

... Eagles linebacker Seth Joyner had 2 pick-sixes and 3 fumble recoveries for touchdowns. His 5 fumble/INT combined TDs is tied for most in team history (Eric Allen, Sheldon Brown).

Oddly enough...

59... Phillies great Chuck Klein had a team-record 59 doubles in 1930.

60

Chuck Bednarik – Eagles/LB-C (1949-62)   Chuck Bednarik was one of the fiercest hitters to ever play in the NFL. Bednarik's stance over a prone New York Giants Frank Gifford is one of the NFL's most iconic images. He was the NFL's last true two-way player and earned the nickname 60-minute Man for his ability to play both sides of the ball (center and linebacker). Bednarik was selected 1st overall by the Eagles in the 1949 NFL Draft. He appeared in an Eagles'-record 8 Pro Bowl games, and was a ten-time 1st Team All Pro. Concrete Charley was very durable, missing only 3 games in the 14 seasons he played. He is 5th on the Eagles all-time games played list. He won two NFL Championships with the Eagles (1949, 1960) and was the 1954 Pro Bowl MVP. He was named to the NFL's 1950's All Decade Team, and the NFL's 75th Anniversary Team. The Maxwell Club in Philadelphia annually presents the Chuck Bednarik Award to the best collegiate defensive player. Bednarik is in the NFL Hall of Fame, Eagles Hall of Fame, and his Eagles #60 was retired.

Did you know...

... Phillies Manager Andy Cohen is the only Phillies Manager with a perfect winning percentage. In 1960, Manager Eddie Sawyer resigned after the first game of the season. The Phillies hired Gene Mauch to replace him but Andy Cohen managed the second game of the season as Mauch arrived a day later. The Phillies beat the Milwaukee Braves 5-4 in 10 innings giving Cohen his one and only managerial win.

... Eagles Hall of Famer Chuck Bednarik holds the team record for games played by an offensive lineman with 169.

Even up...

60... Flyers defenseman Garry Galley holds the team record for assists by a defenseman in one season. Galley notched 60 assists for the Flyers in 1993-94.

60... Eagles QB Nick Foles had a completion pct. of 60.8 in 2012. It was an Eagles rookie record until Carson Wentz topped it in 2016 with a 62.4.

61

Wayne Gomes – Phillies (1997-01) Wayne Gomes debuted for the Phillies in June of 1997. Gomes went 27-21 with a 4.22 ERA in 288 relief appearances. He had 28 saves. During his time with the Reading Phillies, Gomes was the victim of an elaborate prank by pitching coach (now Phillies broadcaster) Larry Andersen. Andersen had the manager in on the prank and hired a Japanese actor for a fake interview. Then they told Gomes he'd been traded to Japan. They recorded the entire gag. At one point, Gomes phones his mother to tell her he'd been traded to Japan.

Steve Everitt – Eagles/C (1997-99) Long-haired, head-banging Steve Everitt played 45 games for the Birds over three years. He had two fumble recoveries. Post-football, while living in Florida, his entire area was devastated by Hurricane Irma. Everitt started a go-fund-me page to help neighbors rebuild.

Stefen Wisniewski – Eagles/G (2016-present) Penn State product Stefen Wisniewski started 11 of the 14 games he played in 2017 and started all three playoff games on the road to the Eagles Super Bowl LII Championship. He is the nephew of Pro Bowler Steve Wisniewski.

Did you know...

... The Flyers won their 2nd consecutive Stanley Cup in May 1975. However, the Flyers only scored 61 goals at home all season. It's their lowest home goal total in team history.

Oddly enough...

61... Flyers sniper Reggie Leach scored a team-record 61 goals during the 1975-76 regular season. He added 19 more in the playoffs.

61... Flyers Legion of Doom winger John LeClair scored a team-record 61 game-winning goals during his Flyers career.

61... Eagles kicker Jake Elliott kicked the longest FG in team history when he booted a 61-yarder on September, 24th, 2017 vs. New York Giants. The Eagles seemed unbeatable from that moment on going all the way to the Super Bowl and defeating the New England Patriots in Super Bowl LII.

62

Jason Kelce – Eagles/C (2011-Present) Jason Kelce will always be a cult hero for legions of Eagles fan after his legendary speech at the Eagles Super Bowl LII Championship victory parade. Dressed in full mummer regalia, Kelce voiced every criticism that had been leveled towards his teammates and embraced the underdog status with the mantra "Hungry Dogs Run Faster." Kelce was 1st Team All Pro for 2017, and a 2014, 2016 Pro Bowler.

Did you know...

... Eagles center Jason Kelce plays the saxophone, and was a standout forward on his high school ice hockey team.

Even up...

62... The Flyers have had 62 penalty shots in their team history. They have scored on 22 of them. Simon Gagne leads the team with 3 goals on 3 penalty shots.

62... The late Flyers D-man Dmitri Tertyshny played 62 games for the Flyers during the 1998-99 season, his only season with the team. Tertyshny died in a tragic boating accident in July of 1999.

62... Nick Foles (10/26/14 vs Arizona Cardinals) and Randall Cunningham (10/2/89 vs Chicago Bears) hold the team record for pass attempts in a single game with 62.

62... Eagles QB Carson Wentz had a rookie-record 62.4 completion pct. in 2016.

62... On November 26th, 1972 the Eagles gave up a team-record 62 points to the New York Giants in a 62-10 defeat. It's their 2nd largest margin of defeat. Their largest margin of defeat also came at the hands of the New York Giants when they lost 56-0 on October 15th, 1933 in their inaugural season.

62... On Christmas Night, 1960, The Sixers (Nationals) defeated the New York Knicks 162-100 for their largest margin of victory in team history (62 points).

62... In 1989 the Eagles defense sacked opposing QBs a team record 62 times in a 16-game season.

63

Ron Baker – Eagles/G (1980-88) Ron Baker was a member of the Eagles Super Bowl XV team that lost to the Oakland Raiders. Baker started 106 games in his 9 seasons with the Birds. Baker touched the football 5 times in his 9 seasons in Philly. He recovered 4 fumbles, and in 1980 had a kick return for 6 yards. Baker once went on the injured reserve list after a freak accident as Baker sliced a tendon in his foot when he slipped in the shower and was cut by a broken tile.

Jake Diekman – Phillies/P (2012-15) Diekman was a hard-throwing lefty reliever that was part of an exciting young Phillies bullpen. That bullpen did not stay together long as Ken Giles was traded for Vince Velasquez and four minor leaguers, and Diekman was traded along with Cole Hamels to Texas in a move that brought several top prospects (Jorge Alfaro, Jerad Eickhoff, Jake Thompson, and Nick Williams). Diekman's 96+ mph fastball is among the best of all MLB lefty relievers.

Oddly enough...

63... Bobby Wine was the 1st Phillies player to win a Gold Glove Award, winning it in 1963.

63... On October 16th, 1963 the Philadelphia 76ers played their first game since relocating from Syracuse. The Sixers defeated the Detroit Pistons in Detroit, 117-115.

63... On October 19th, 1963 the Philadelphia 76ers played their first home game as a Philadelphia franchise, losing to the Detroit Pistons 124-121.

64

Ed Blaine – Eagles/G (1963-66) Blaine won a Super Bowl under Vince Lombardi with the Green Bay Packers in 1962. He joined the Eagles in 1963 and was All Pro in 1964. During his off-seasons, Blaine was finishing up his PHd. After five seasons in the NFL, Blaine left to go into medicine. Dr. Blaine devoted his professional career to studying hypertension. He has several patents for discovering ACE inhibitors (Angiotensin converting enzyme inhibitors).

Did you know...

... The 1964 Phillies team that blew a 6 ½ game lead with 12 games to go committed an insane 17 errors during the collapse.

... On April 16th, 2018, Phillies relief pitcher Victor Arano threw a perfect 8th inning vs Atlanta Braves in a 2-1 loss, getting 3 outs on 3 pitches. The outs were the 20th, 21st, and 22nd consecutive outs (6 appearances) for Arano to start the 2018 season.

Even up...

64... On November 6th, 1934 the Eagles defeated the Cincinnati Reds 64-0. It's the most points in a game for the Eagles and their largest margin of victory in team history.

64... On July 7th, 1964 Phillies slugger Johnny Callison was the MLB All Star Game MVP, becoming the 1st and still only Phillies player to ever win it.

64... Phillies infielder Ruben Amaro sr. won a Gold Glove in 1964.

64... Phillies outfielder Richie Allen was the NL Rookie of the Year in 1964.

65

Lane Johnson – Eagles/T (2013-Present) Lane Johnson was selected by the Eagles 4th overall in the 2013 NFL Draft. He was named to the 2017 Pro Bowl Team, 1st Team All Pro, and was a member of the Eagles Super Bowl LII championship team. Lane Johnson and teammate Chris Long started the dog mask craze when the Eagles were picked as underdogs in their opening home playoff game vs Atlanta Falcons. In 2016 Johnson was suspended by the NFL for ten games stemming from his second PED violation. Johnson denies using the PED and a lawsuit is ongoing.

Charlie Johnson – Eagles/T (1977-81) Charlie Johnson was the starting nose tackle for the Eagles Super Bowl XV team that lost to the Oakland Raiders. Johnson was a three-time Pro Bowler with the Eagles, and a two-time All Pro. Johnson had 7 fumble recoveries for the Eagles, and had three interceptions in 1980.

Did you know...

... Eagles Pro Bowl tackle Lane Johnson's father-in-law is John Goodman, a defensive end for the Pittsburgh Steelers 1980-85.

Oddly enough...

65... DeSean Jackson returned a Matt Dodge punt 65 yards for a touchdown as time expired capping off a miraculous comeback win over the New York Giants. The "Miracle of the Meadowlands II," on December 19th, 2010 saw the Eagles score 28 points in the final seven minutes and twenty-eight seconds. DeSean Jackson became the first player in NFL history to run back a punt for a touchdown to win a game as time expired. In 2013, NFL.com readers voted Jackson's TD return the greatest play of all-time (over 58 million votes).

65... Eagles QB Sam Bradford has the best career pass-completion pct. in team history at 65.0.

65... The Flyers have had two players wear the #65 sweater in team history, Nate Guenin in 2007 and Kyle Greentree in 2008. Though they played just 14 games collectively for the orange and black, the two #65's averaged 65 minutes of total ice time in their Flyers career.

66

Bill Bergey – Eagles/LB (1974-80) Bill Bergey is widely regarded as one of the NFL's all-time greatest linebackers not in the Hall of Fame. Bergey was a mainstay on the Eagles defense and helped to catapult them to a Super Bowl XV appearance. Bergey was a four-time Pro Bowler, two-time 1st Team All Pro, and led the NFL in fumble recoveries in 1975. His 15 defensive fumble recoveries is tied for 4th best in team history. Bergey had 18 INTs with the Birds and set an NFL record for most INTs by a linebacker. Bergey was a three-time Eagles MVP, inducted into the Philly Sports Hall of Fame, and entered the Eagles Hall of Fame in 1988.

Yanick Dupre – Flyers/LW (1991-96) Yanick Dupre was a left winger selected 50th overall by the Flyers in the 1991 NHL Entry Draft. Six years later, after having played in 35 NHL games for the Flyers, Dupre lost his 16-month battle with leukemia. In 1999, the Flyers redefined their "Class Guy Award," and renamed it the "Yanick Dupre Memorial Class Guy Award." The award is given annually to the Flyer who best illustrates character, dignity and respect for the sport, on and off the ice. The American Hockey League, where Yanick Dupre played 207 games as a Flyer prospect for the Hershey Bears, annually presents the "Yanick Dupre Memorial Award" for the AHL's Man of the Year for service to his local community.

Even up...

66... On February 8th, 1966, the NHL granted Ed Snider and Philadelphia a conditional franchise to begin play during the 1967-68 season. The Flyers were born!

66... Eagles Kimo Von Oelhoffen was born in Kaunakakai, Hawaii. His full name is Kimo Kukuiokalani von Oelhoffen.

67

Jamaal Jackson – Eagles/C (2003-11) Jamaal Jackson spent nine seasons with the Eagles at Center. The 330-pounder signed with the Eagles after going undrafted out of Delaware State. Jackson beat out incumbent Hank Fraley for the starting job, and eventually lost it to Jason Kelce. The three centers covered the Eagles at that position for nearly 18 years. Jackson battled injuries during his career but was selected by Sports Illustrated for 2006 All Pro honors.

Oddly enough...

67... On June 5th, 1967 the NHL officially expanded from 6 to 12 teams adding the Flyers, Pittsburgh Penguins, California Seals, Los Angeles Kings, Minnesota North Stars and St. Louis Blues to begin play in October 1967. The following day the Flyers selected Bernie Parent with their 1st expansion pick.

67... The Flyers played their 1st NHL game on October 11th, 1967, a 5-1 loss in Oakland. They notched their 1st ever win on October 18th, 1967, a 2-1 win in St. Louis. The next night they won their very first home game, a 1-0 shutout over the visiting Pittsburgh Penguins.

67... Though the Flyers went 7-1-2 vs St. Louis Blues during the 1967-68 NHL regular season, the Flyers lost to them in the 1st round of the playoffs 4 games to 3 in their 1st-ever playoff series.

68

Jaromir Jagr – Flyers/RW (2011-12) Jaromir Jagr, at 39 years of age, was already one of the greatest hockey players of all time when he decided to return to the NHL, signing a one year contract to play for the Flyers in 2011. Jagr scored his 1600th point in his first game for the orange and black. Jagr played 73 games with the Flyers that season netting 19 goals with 35 assists for 54 points. Only Claude Giroux (93) and Scott Hartnell (67) had more points for the Flyers that season. Jagr scored another 8 points in 11 playoff contests. Two of Jagr's teammates (Sean Couturier and Brayden Schenn) hadn't even been born when Jagr made his NHL debut with the Pittsburgh Penguins. The Flyers declined to resign the 40 year old Jagr after the 2011-12 season. All Jagr did was play another 387 games and score another 101 goals after leaving the Flyers. I'll have what he's drinking!

Did you know...

... The Sixers had a team-record 68 wins during the 1966-67 regular season leading up to their 1966-67 NBA Championship.

Even up...

68... Hall of Famer Wilt Chamberlain scored a Sixers team-record 68 points in a 143-123 victory over the Chicago Bulls on December 16th, 1967.

68... On April 4th, 1968 the Flyers played their 1st playoff game in team history, a 1-0 loss to the St. Louis Blues.

68... On April 6th, 1968 the Flyers recorded their 1st playoff win defeating the visiting St. Louis Blues 4-3.

69

Jon Runyan – Eagles/T (2000-2008) Jon Runyan was big, fierce, and dirty, and wreaked havoc on opposing players in the NFL. As if that wasn't bad enough for the other team, he once played 190 consecutive games. That's a lot of punishment. Runyan was a 2000 free agent signing for the Eagles and at the time of his signing, he was the highest paid offensive lineman in NFL history. Runyan was a 2002 Pro Bowler, and a member of the Eagles Super Bowl XXXIX team. Runyan was named to the Eagles 75th Anniversary Team. After his football days, Runyan served four years in the US Congress from New Jersey's 3rd district. Need a lift? Runyan sometimes moonlights as an Uber driver.

Evan Mathis – Eagles/G (2011-14) Evan Mathis was a force on the Eagles' front line for four seasons. While in Philly, Mathis was a two-time Pro Bowler, a 1st Team All Pro, and was rated by Football Focus as the best guard in the NFL for 2011, 2012, 2013. Mathis held out of OTAs in 2015 in a contract dispute and was released by the team.

Did you know...

... Eagles tackle Jon Runyan was a two-time shot putter state champ in HS. Runyan was also the last active player to play for the Houston Oilers.

... Eagles tackle Jon Runyan appeared in an episode of the TV show "It's Always Sunny in Philadelphia".

70

Al Wistert – Eagles/T (1944-51) Al Wistert played his entire 9-year career with the Eagles. His rookie year was spent on the Steagles (the joint Philadelphia–Pittsburgh team during WWII). Wistert spent five seasons as team captain. He played in the first-ever Pro Bowl in 1950. Wistert was an eight-time NFL All Pro. He was a member of the Eagles back-to-back Championship teams in 1948, 1949. He was named to the 1940's All-Decade Team. The Eagles retired his #70 in 1952, and he entered the Eagles Hall of Fame in 2009.

Even up...

70... Phillies relief pitcher Billy Wagner finished a team-record 70 games during the 2005 MLB season.

70... In 1992, the Phillies won 70 games. It's the only 70-win season in their 136 years. Winning 70 games that year also meant they lost 92 in '92.

70... The Phillies have had only two 70-loss seasons in their history. They went 92-70 in their World Series Championship season of 2008, and they went 92-70 in 1964, the year of the great collapse.

71

Jason Peters – Eagles/T (2009-Present) Jason Peters has been a dominant OT for the Eagles for a decade. During his time with the Birds, he's been a seven-time Pro Bowler, three-time 1st Team All Pro, and a 2nd Team All Pro in 2010. The future Hall of Famer was undrafted out of college and signed with the Buffalo Bills as a free agent in 2004 as a TE! Peters was a member of the Eagles Super Bowl LII championship team but went down with a season-ending knee injury in week #7.

Ken Clarke – Eagles/T (1978-87) Nose Tackle Ken Clarke spent ten seasons with the Birds. He was a member of the Eagles Super Bowl XV team. Ken Clarke didn't miss a game in eight of his ten seasons with the Birds. Clarke had 10.5 sacks in 1984. He is 12th on the Eagles all-time list in games played with 148, and 13th with 32.5 career sacks.

Did you know…

… On June 23rd, 1971, Phillies pitcher Rick Wise threw a no-hitter vs Cincinnati Reds, giving up just one walk. Wise hit 2 HRs in the game becoming the first pitcher in MLB history to hit 2 HRs while throwing a no-hitter.

… Phillies 1B Deron Johnson hit a career-high 34 HRs for the Phillies in 1971.

Oddly enough...

71... All four Philadelphia teams had losing records for 1971. Only the Eagles were close to a .500 record (6-7-1). The Phils were 67-95, Flyers 26-38-14, and the Sixers were 30-52. The collective .406 winning pct was bad, but the following season was historical (collective .332 winning pct.).

72

Tra Thomas – Eagles/T (1998-08 player, 2013-14 coach) Tra Thomas was the 11th overall pick in the 1998 NFL Draft. Thomas was 2nd Team All Pro in 2002, and a Pro Bowler in 2001, 2002, and 2004. Thomas was the starting left tackle for the Eagles Super Bowl XXXIX team. For the 2006 and 2007 season Thomas requested he be referred to by his given name "William Thomas." In 2008 he went back to "Tra." Thomas played 166 games for the Eagles, 6th-most in franchise history. Thomas was named to the Eagles 75th Anniversary Team.

Wade Key – Eagles/T (1970-79) Wade Key's career with the Eagles touched three decades. He was drafted by the Birds in 1969 NFL Draft, and was waived by the team in September of 1980. In between, Key played 121 games, had four fumble recoveries, and in 2007 was named to the Eagles 75th Anniversary Team.

Did you know...

... Phillies legend Mike Schmidt made his MLB debut on September 12th, 1972.

... Eagles T Halapoulivaati Vaitai is of Tongan descent but was born in Texas. He also has the longest first name in Eagles history.

... Eagle T Wade Key was drafted by the Birds in the 13th round of the 1969 NFL Draft. He was the 314th player selected.

Even up...

72... Phillies infielder Juan Samuel had a team modern-day record 72 stolen bases during the 1984 season, the most for a Phillies player since 1895.

72... In 1972, Philly sports suffered historic futility. The four teams went a collective 107-211-12 for a .332 winning pct., the worst for any 4 sport city in North America. Ever! The Sixers were an NBA worst-ever 9-73, the Phillies lost 95 games, and the Eagles were 2-11-1. The Flyers winning season, 37-30-11 was not enough to keep the city out of the record books.

73

Shawn Andrews – Eagles/G (2004-09) Shawn Andrews had several strong seasons with the Eagles, going to the Pro Bowl twice and being named a 1st Team All Pro. A leg injury in the 2004 season opener derailed Andrews for the Eagles NFC Championship season. Andrews dealt with depression and chronic back issues that kept him out for most of his last two seasons with the Eagles. Though his brother Stacy joined the Birds in 2009, they never made it into a game together as Eagles. Andrews was named to the Eagles 75th Anniversary Team.

Ed Khayat – Eagles/DT (1958-61, 64-65 as player, 1971-72 head coach) Ed Khayat was the starting DT for the Eagles 1960 NFL Championship Team. Khayat became the 12th Head Coach in Eagles history 3 games into the 1971 season. He went 2-11-1 the following season, his last as an NFL Head Coach. He finished with a 8-15-2 record for the Birds.

Broad Street Bullies...

... Philadelphia Bulletin sportswriter Jack Chevalier, in an article printed on January 3rd, 1973 called the Flyers 'the Mean Machine', 'Freddy's Phillistines' and the 'Bullies of Broad Street.' Pete Cafone wrote the headline 'Broad Street Bullies Muscle Atlanta'. The nickname stuck!

Did you know...

... On St. Patrick's Day 1973, the Sixers lost their 68th game of the season, setting an NBA record for losses in a season. The 1970-71 Cleveland Cavaliers and the 1967-68 Houston Rockets held the previous record of 67 losses. The Sixers record loss was a 120-115 defeat at home to the Baltimore Bullets. The Sixers finished with an NBA-record 73 losses and only 9 wins.

Oddly enough...

73... During the 1966-67 the Sixers scored 100+ points a team-record 73 consecutive games.

73... The 1972-73 Sixers team lost an NBA-record 73 games (9-73). During the season they won back to back games twice. They lost their first 15 games, and their last 13 games of the season.

73... Flyers Hall of Fame goalie Bernie Parent played a team-record 73 games in net for the Flyers in 1973-74.

74

Mike Pitts – Eagles/DT (1987-92) Mike Pitts played 75 of his 169 career NFL games for the Eagles. Pitts was the starting left DT for the Eagles infamous Gang Green team in 1991. His 19.5 sacks ranks 25th on the Eagles all-time list, and his 397 tackles ranks him 11th.

Did you know...

... On May 19th, 1974 the Flyers won their 1st Stanley Cup in team history defeating the Boston Bruins 1-0 to win the series 4 games to 2. It was the 1st Stanley Cup won by an expansion team in league history.

... The 1973-74 Stanley Cup Finals between the Flyers and Boston Bruins featured 6 future Hall of Famers (Bill Barber, Bobby Clarke, and Bernie Parent for the Flyers... Johnny Bucyk, Phil Esposito and Bobby Orr for the Bruins).

... Flyers Rick MacLeish scored the Cup-winning goal in the 1973-74 Stanley Cup Finals vs Boston Bruins. It gave him his 13th playoff goal and 22nd playoff point, tops in the playoffs that season.

... During the Flyers run to their 1st Stanley Cup in 1974, Flyers Don "Big Bird" Saleski led the team with a +9 for the playoffs.

Even up...

74... On November 28th, 1985 Eagles RB Herman Hunter rushed 74 yards for a TD vs Dallas Cowboys. It's the longest rookie rushing TD in team history.

75

Stan Walters – Eagles/T (1975-83) Stan Walters was a hulking 6'6" 275lb blocking machine for Wilbert Montgomery. Walters was a two-time Pro Bowler. He started every game from 1975-82, a string of 122 consecutive starts. Walters retired prior to the start of the 1983 season but came back and played 12 games. After he retired again at the end of the season, Walters joined Merrill Reese as part of the Eagles radio broadcast team from 1985-97. Walters entered the Eagles Hall of Fame in 1999.

Did you know...

... In 1975 Terry Rocap, Joe Sherwood, and Randy Childress recorded the song "Here Come the Sixers." The tune was very popular at the time. 1,2,3,4,5,Sixers... 10,9,8,76ers! Indeed!

Oddly enough...

75... Phillies Secretary of Defense Garry Maddox won the 1st of his 8 Gold Glove Awards with the Phillies in 1975.

75... On May 27th, 1975 the Flyers defeated the Buffalo Sabres 2-0 in game six of the Stanley Cup Final to win their 2nd consecutive Stanley Cup Championship.

75... Eagles Steve Van Buren (1944-51) and Reggie White (1985-92) were the only two Eagles named to the NFL's 75th Anniversary Team in 1994. Chuck Bednarik, Bill Hewitt, Pete Pihos, and Steve Van Buren were included on the All 2-way team for players playing both sides of the ball.

76

Jerry Sisemore – Eagles/G-T (1973-84) Jerry Sisemore was one of the all-time greatest offensive linemen in Eagles history. He was a difference-maker that helped the Eagles to four consecutive playoff appearances including Super Bowl XV. Sisemore was selected 3rd overall by the Eagles in the 1973 draft. The two-time Pro Bowler is 10th in games played for the Eagles, having started 127 of them consecutively. Sisemore entered the Eagles Hall of Fame in 1991.

Bob Brown – Eagles/T (1964-68) Bob Brown was taken 2nd overall by the Eagles in the 1964 NFL Draft. Brown was a three-time Pro Bowler and three-time All Pro during his five seasons with the Eagles. Boomer was named to the all-1960's team, and entered the Eagles Hall of Fame in 2004. Brown was inducted in the Pro Football Hall of Fame in 2004.

Shawn Bradley – Sixers/C (1993-95) Shawn Bradley was drafted by the Sixers 2nd overall in the 1993 NBA draft. Bradley was named to the NBA All-Rookie 2nd team in 1994. At 7'6", Bradley was the third tallest player in NBA history (Gheorghe Muresan, Manute Bol). Bradley's 274 blocks in his second season is a Sixers record.

Did you know...

... Sixers Shawn Bradley appeared in the movie "Space Jam",
and an episode of the TV show "Walker, Texas Ranger".

... Sixers big man Shawn Bradley grew up in Utah but was born
in Landstuhl, West Germany.

Even up...

76... Sixers great Allen Iverson had a team-record 76 40+ point
games during his Sixers career.

76... Flyers Reggie Leach scored an NHL-record 19 goals in the
1976 Stanley Cup playoffs.

77

Paul Coffey – Flyers/D (1996-98) Paul Coffey was one of the greatest offensive defensemen in NHL history. The Hall of Famer spent a season and a half with the Flyers in the later stages of his career, and helped the Flyers to the 1997 Stanley Cup Final. Coffey was knocked out of the Finals in the second game of the series with a concussion. Coffey holds over 30 NHL career, regular season, and playoff records. Coffey was inducted into the Hockey Hall of Fame in 2004.

Did you know...

... Hall of Fame defenseman Paul Coffey was once traded along with Sylvain Couturier, the father of Flyers Sean Couturier.

... Eagles offensive lineman Antone Davis was on the 12th season of TV's "The Biggest Loser."

Oddly enough...

77... Flyers Hall of Famer Bobby Clarke holds the Flyers team record for postseason assists with 77 during his Flyers career.

77... Eagles great Steve Van Buren had a team-record 77 career rushing TDs.

78

Carl Hairston – Eagles/DE (1976-1983) Carl "Big Daddy" Hairston was a solid defensive end who played 8 seasons with the Eagles. Hairston was part of the Eagles Dick Vermeil-led Super Bowl XV team. Hairston played a total of 15 NFL seasons before moving into coaching for another 15 seasons. Hairston played for Dick Vermeil, and then coached with him. Hairston won a Super Bowl as part of Dick Vermeil's Super Bowl XXXIV-winning St. Louis Rams.

Hollis Thomas – Eagles/DT (1996-05) Hollis Thomas was signed as an undrafted free agent. He has said that going undrafted drove him to be the best he could be in his NFL career. He was a significant contributor for 9 seasons with the Birds. Tank played 126 games for the Eagles (30th on their all-time list). He is tied for 13th on the Eagles with 7 forced fumbles, 30th in sacks (13.5) and 18th in tackles (288). Tank was a member of the Eagles Super Bowl XXXIX team.

Marion Campbell – Eagles/DT-T (1956-61 as a player, 1977-82 defensive coordinator, 1983-85 Head Coach) Marion Campbell wore many hats during his Eagles career. He was a two-time Pro Bowler and a 1st team All Pro during the Eagles 1960 NFL Championship season. The Swamp Fox was one of the last of a breed in that he played both sides of the ball. After his playing days, Campbell turned to coaching where he excelled as a defensive coordinator. His defenses helped the Eagles to a Super Bowl XV appearance. The Eagles defense for the 1980 and 1981 seasons were ranked 1st or 2nd in fewest points and fewest yards given up both seasons. The Swamp Fox did not fare nearly as well as Head Coach. His career head coaching record is the 5th worst in NFL history for coaches with a minimum of 5 seasons.

Even up...

78... Phillies legend Robin Roberts was inducted into the Phillies Wall of Fame in 1978.

78... Phillies slugger Greg Luzinski won the Roberto Clemente Award in 1978.

78... Phillies catcher Bob Boone won his first of two Gold Glove Awards in 1978.

79

Todd Herremans – Eagles/T (2005-14) On November 2nd, 2008, vs Seattle Seahawks, tackle Todd Herremans became the first Eagle offensive lineman in 74 years to catch a TD pass when he snagged a 1-yd TD pass from Donovan McNabb. On December 12, 2010 vs Dallas Cowboys, Herremans caught a 2-yard Mike Vick pass for his 2nd career TD. Herremans played 127 games for the Birds over ten seasons, 28th on Eagles all-time list.

Brandon Brooks – Eagles/G (2016-Present) Brandon Brooks signed with the Eagles as a free agent in 2016. He missed the first two games of the season dealing with anxiety issues. Brooks had his best season to date in 2017 earning his first Pro Bowl nod. He started all 16 regular season games and 3 post season games. Brooks was a member of the Eagles Super Bowl LII Championship Team.

Did you know...

... Eagles G Brandon Brooks attended the wedding of an Eagles fan and fellow Miami of Ohio alum prior to the 2017 season. The fan had written to Brooks, inviting him to his nuptials. Brooks accepted.

Oddly enough...

79... Eagles great Harold Carmichael had a team-record 79 career receiving touchdowns, the most for any receiver in team history.

79... Eagles QB Carson Wentz has the best rookie QB passer rating in team history with a 79.3 rating in 2016. Nick Foles is 2nd best with a 79.1 in 2012.

80

Cris Carter – Eagles/WR (1987-89) Cris Carter could easily be classified as the one that got away. Buddy Ryan saw the potential in Carter, but Carter's battles with drugs and alcohol during his time with the Eagles prompted Ryan to release the would-be star. Carter then signed with the Vikings, and the rest, as they say, was history. Carter got his act together and went on to have a Hall of Fame career with the Vikings, playing in 8 consecutive Pro Bowls. The Vikings retired his #80. Upon Buddy Ryan's death, Carter thanked Ryan for saving his life with tough love.

Irving Fryar – Eagles/WR (1996-98) Irving Fryar was born in Mount Holly, NJ and attended Rancocas Valley HS. Fryar was selected #1 overall by the New England Patriots in the 1984 NFL Draft, just the second wide receiver ever taken with the top pick. Fryar played just 3 of his 17 NFL seasons with the Eagles, but went to two of his five Pro Bowls while with the Birds. Fryar was awarded the Bart Starr Man of the Year Award in 1998, his last year in Philly. On October 20th, 1996 vs. Miami Dolphins, Fryar had a team-tying record 4 TD catches. He is the oldest NFL player to have 4 TD catches in one game. Fryar had 11 TD catches in his first season with the Eagles, the most he had in any season in his career. Fryar had legal issues post-NFL, and was sentenced to five years in prison for his part in a real estate scam.

Did you know...

... Eagles Irving Fryar played 255 games in his 17-season NFL career, the most ever by a New Jersey native.

Even up...

80... In 1980, all four of Philly's major sports teams appeared in their respective championship games/series. The Eagles lost Super Bowl XV to the Oakland Raiders, the Flyers lost the Stanley Cup Finals to the New York Islanders, and the Sixers lost the NBA Finals to the Los Angeles Lakers. The Phillies were the only team of the four to win, beating the Kansas City Royals for their first World Series Championship.

80... Eagles punter Donnie Jones holds the team record for games played by a punter with 80.

80... The 1984-85 Sixers had a team-record 80.3 free throw pct.

80... The Sixers have scored 100+ points in a game 80 times in one season, twice. In 1966-67, they hit 100+ points in every game except 11/5/66 vs Boston where they were held to 87. In 1969-70 the Sixers scored 100+ points in every game except 10/25/69, held to 98 vs Cincinnati, and 11/21/69 where they were held to 94 vs New York.

81

Terrell Owens – Eagles/WR (2004-05) Terrell Owens spent a season and a half in Philly. It was a wild ride. In 2004, Terrell Owens had one of the best single seasons in Eagles history. He had 77 catches for 1200 yards, and 14 TDs in 14 games. He was selected for the Pro Bowl and was a 1st team All Pro. Owens broke his fibula and damaged ligaments in his ankle during a week 15 win over the Dallas Cowboys. Miraculously, 7 weeks later he was playing in Super Bowl XXXIX. He had 9 catches for 122 yards in the Super Bowl in a losing effort. Afterward, Owens insinuated that QB Donovan McNabb was tired and cost the Eagles the Super Bowl. It was the beginning of the end for Owens in Philly. The ever-outspoken Owens was unhappy with his 7-year contract and wanted to renegotiate. He became a distraction. T.O. only played 7 games for the Birds in '05, and before we knew it he was doing sit-ups in his driveway for the press. Owens was released at the end of the season. T.O.'s nickname should have been "the enigma." He feuded with the 49ers, feuded with Donovan McNabb and the Eagles, once pulled out a sharpie to autograph a football he just scored a TD with, yet has done tremendous charity work in the fight against Alzheimer's, written a children's book, a fitness book, developed a men's luxury clothing line, and competed on Dancing with the Stars. He was inducted into the Pro Football Hall of Fame in 2018.

Did you know...

... Eagles Hall of Fame receiver Terrell Owens had a team-record seven 100-yard receiving games in 2004, 5 of which were consecutive (also a team record).

Oddly enough...

81.... The Eagles made their first Super Bowl appearance in 1981, appearing in Super Bowl XV against the Oakland Raiders on January 25th. The Raiders won 27-10.

82

Mike Quick – Eagles/WR (1982-90) Mike Quick was simply one of the greatest receivers in Eagles history. The five-time Pro Bowler and two-time 1st Team All Pro, led the NFL in receiving yards in 1983 (1409) and was 2nd in 1985 (1247). Quick is 3rd on the Eagles all-time list for career receiving yards (6464), and 3rd in receiving TDs (61). On November 10th, 1985 vs. Atlanta Falcons, Ron Jaworski threw a 29-yard toss to Quick who then ran 70 yards for a TD and an overtime win. The 99-yard TD pass is tied for the longest in NFL history. Quick is currently the color analyst for the Eagles radio broadcasts. He entered the Eagles Hall of Fame in 1995.

LJ Smith – Eagles/TE (2003-08) LJ Smith was a talented tight end for the Birds. Little John scored the Eagles first touchdown in Super Bowl XXXIX. Smith is 7th all-time on the Eagles list for reception % (non-RB) with a minimum 100 catches. He is 27th in Eagles history in TD receptions, 28th in Rec Yards, and 22nd in receptions.

Did you know...

... Eagles LJ Smith appeared in Campbell's Chunky Soup commercials with Donovan McNabb.

... 1969 Eagles Pro Bowler Tim Rossovich was the college roommate of actor Tom Selleck. After football, Rossovich appeared in over 30 TV shows, including three episodes of Magnum, PI., and several notable movies.

Even up...

82... Flyers Legion of Doom winger Mikael Renberg holds the team record for points by a rookie, notching 82 points during the 1993-94 season.

82... Flyers Hall of Famer Mark Howe holds the team record for points in a season by a defenseman with 82 points in 1985-86.

83

Vince Papale – Eagles/WR (1976-78) Vince Papale, at 30 years old, was the oldest non-kicker rookie in NFL history to never have played college football. The 2006 Mark Wahlberg movie "Invincible" was based on Papale's improbable road to the NFL. Papale did attend college but went to St. Joe's on a scholarship for track and field. They did not have a football program. Papale was a walk-on to start his professional career, but it was with the Philadelphia Bell of the WFL, not the Eagles. Papale was invited to try out by Dick Vermeil based on his play with the Bell. Once an Eagle, Papale was picked to be the Special Teams captain by his teammates. He was recognized for his charitable work when he was named Eagles Man of the Year in 1978. Papale was named to the Eagles 75th Anniversary Team.

Did you know...

... Eagles Mr. Invincible, Vince Papale, had more career fumble recoveries than receptions. He had two fumble recoveries and only one reception off a Roman Gabriel pass for 15 yards (vs. Tampa Bay Buccaneers).

... Eagle kicker/receiver Bobby Walston once scored 25 points in a single game. On October 17th, 1954 vs. Washington Redskins, Walston scored three TDs (18 points) and had 7 PATs (7 points) in an Eagles 49-21 win.

... Eagle Kicker David Akers is 1st on the Eagles all-time scoring list with 1,323 points. Kicker/receiver Bobby Walston is 2nd with 881 points. Walston scored 46 TDs, 80 FGs, 365 PATs. Akers had 882 points on FGs alone.

... Eagles WR Greg Lewis is the only receiver in NFL history to have a 30+ yard reception in 3 consecutive playoff games after having zero during the regular season.

84

Keith Krepfle – Eagles/TE (1975-81) Keith Krepfle stood in the shadows of Charle Young during his first two seasons with the Birds. When Young was traded for Ron Jaworski, it was a double-win for Krepfle. Four years later, the two connected for the only Eagles TD in their Super Bowl XV loss. Krepfle was a 1st Team All Pro in 1979 and finished his Eagles career with 151 catches for 2,420 yards and 19 TDs (23rd on Eagles all-time receiving TD list).

Freddie Mitchell – Eagles/WR (2001-04) Freddie Mitchell played his entire four-year career with the Eagles. FredEx liked to be provocative. From his frohawk, to pointing to his watch after a catch as if to say 'about time', or during a press conference, thanking his hands for being great, Mitchell was never at a loss. He is most remembered, however, for the infamous 4th and 26. On January 11th, 2004 in a playoff game vs. Green Bay Packers, Mitchell caught a 28-yard Donovan McNabb pass on a 4th and 26 play with the game on the line and the Eagles trailing by 3. The catch was huge and extended the Eagles drive which led to tying the game and winning it in overtime, sending the Eagles to the NFC Championship game vs Carolina Panthers.

Did you know...

... Eagles TE Keith Krepfle caught the Eagle's very first Super Bowl TD, an 8-yard catch from Ron Jaworski in Super Bowl XV on January 25th, 1981 in a 27-10 loss to the Oakland Raiders. It stood as the Eagles only Super Bowl TD reception for 23 years.

... Eagles WR Freddie Mitchell and RB Rod Smart are first cousins and were 2001 Eagles teammates.

... The Flyers scored a team-record 350 goals during the 1983-84 season.

Even up...

84... Flyers goalie Ron Hextall played in 84 postseason games for the Flyers during his career, the most for any goalie in team history. He tied an NHL record for games by a goalie in one playoff season when he played 26 games for the Flyers in his rookie season 1987. The Flyers lost in the Stanley Cup Finals to the Edmonton Oilers but Hextall was the Conn Smythe Winner for MVP of the playoffs.

84... On December 22nd, 2013, Eagles QB Nick Foles went 21 for 25 in passing for a team-record 84.0 single game completion pct.

85

Charles Smith – Eagles/WR (1974-81) Charlie Smith played his entire 8-year NFL career with the Eagles. Smith had a career 218 receptions (27th on Eagles all-time list) for 3,349 yards (18th team best). Smith is 16th on Eagles all-time list with 24 receiving TDs, and there are only 27 Eagles all-time who have played more than the 118 games Smith has played.

Did you know...

... The 1984-85 Flyers that went to the Stanley Cup Finals against the Edmonton Oilers was the youngest team in professional sports that year. While the powerhouse Oilers had 6 future Hall of Famers on their roster, and zero rookies, the Flyers had 4 rookies (Todd Bergen, Rick Tocchet, Derrick Smith, and Peter Zezel) and one future Hall of Famer (Mark Howe).

... The Flyers 1984-85 Stanley Cup Finals series vs Edmonton Oilers was the 1st Stanley Cup Finals with games scheduled into June. The series, however, ended on May 30th as the Oilers won 4 games to 1.

... The 1984-85 Stanley Cup Finals featuring the Flyers and the Edmonton Oilers was the last Finals in NHL history to feature a goalie in the full plexiglass goaltender mask. Both Pelle Lindbergh (Flyers) and Grant Fuhr (Oilers) wore them.

Oddly enough...

85... Flyers Hall of Famer Mark Howe holds the NHL record for single season plus/minus by an American-born defenseman with a +85 in 1985-86.

85... The Flyers battled the powerhouse Edmonton Oilers in the spring of 1985 in the Stanley Cup Finals. The Flyers fell to the Wayne Gretzky-led dynastic Oilers 4 games to 1. The Flyers were outscored 21-14 during the 5 games.

85... Flyers goalie Pelle Lindbergh won his 1st and only Vezina Trophy, and Flyers Head Coach Mike Keenan won the Jack Adams Award as Coach of the Year for the 1984-85 NHL season.

86

Fred Barnett – Eagles/WR (1990-95) Arkansas Fred Barnett was an acrobatic big-play receiver who played 6 seasons with the Eagles. In just his 12th professional game, Barnett caught a pass at the 50-yard line from a scrambling Randall Cunningham who was five yards deep in his own end zone, and raced for a 95-yard touchdown catch. It's the 2nd longest pass play in Eagles history. Barnett was a 1992 Pro Bowler. Barnett is currently 11th on the Eagles all-time list with 4,634 receiving yards, 14th in receiving TDs with 28, and 12th in receptions with 308.

Zach Ertz – Eagles/TE (2013-Present) Zach Ertz is a gifted receiver and a big part of the Eagles drive to their Super Bowl LII championship. He was a 2017 Pro Bowler. Ertz caught 7 passes for 67 yards and a TD in Super Bowl LII. Ertz has only been with the team since 2013 and is already ranked 13th all-time for Eagles receiving TDs with 29. His 437 receptions ranks 3rd, and his 4,827 receiving yards ranks 9th. He was the team's offensive MVP for 2017. On December 23rd, 2018 in a 32-30 win over the Houston Texans, Ertz became the NFL's all-time single-season reception leader for tight ends when he caught a 9-yd Nick Foles pass for his 111th catch of the season. Ertz finished the season with a record 116 catches.

Charle Young – Eagles/TE (1973-76) Charle Young was selected 6th overall by the Eagles in the 1973 NFL Draft. Young was the 1973 UPI

Rookie of the Year. Young played the first 4 of his 13 NFL seasons with the Eagles during which time he was selected to his three Pro Bowls, two 1st Team All-Pros, and one 2nd Team All-Pro. Young was 4th in the NFL in receptions in 1973, and 2nd in 1974. His 80-yard reception in 1973 was the second longest catch in the NFL that season. Young's 2,583 receiving yards is 26th on Eagles all-time list.

Did you know...

... The 1986 Eagles, during Buddy Ryan's debut season, gave up an NFL-record 104 sacks. It was 26 more than the previous record of 78. The Eagles gave up at least three sacks in all 16 games that season, another NFL record.

... Eagles WR Fred Barnett was married in Maasai Mara, Kenya, by the village chief in 2009.

... Eagles TE Zach Ertz is married to Julie Johnston Ertz, a professional soccer player and the starting centerback on the Women's US National Team.

... Eagles TE Zach Ertz had a team-record 15 receptions on December 20th, 2014 vs Washington Redskins.

Even up...

86... The Sixers (Nationals) had a team-record 86 1st half points in a 148-122 win over the Detroit Pistons on February 12th, 1961.

87

Brent Celek – Eagles/TE (2007-18) Brent Celek was a hard-nosed, durable tight end who spent 11 seasons with the Birds. Celek is 4th all-time on the Eagles list for receptions (398) and games played (175). Celek only missed one game in his entire 11-year career with the Eagles. Celek had the 8th most receiving yards and 11th most receiving TDs in team history. Celek had the 2nd best season receiving yards total of any Eagle TE in team history (Pete Retzlaff). Celek's 19 receptions during the 2008-09 playoff season were third most for any TE in NFL history. Celek was a member of the Eagles Super Bowl LII Championship team. Celek was the longest tenured athlete in Philly sports at the time of his release in March 2018.

Donald Brashear – Flyers/LW (2002-06) Donald Brashear was a hard-knuckled throwback that played three and a half seasons in the orange and black. Brashear joined the Flyers halfway through the 2001-02 season and reached his highest career point total. Brash had his second-highest point total of his career during his first full season with the Flyers and was awarded the Pelle Lindbergh Memorial Award. While a member of the Vancouver Canucks, Brashear was once slashed in the head by Boston Bruin Marty McSorley during the 1999-2000 season, resulting in an on-ice seizure. McSorley said he was trying to slash Brashear in the shoulder to get him to fight. The slash effectively ended

McSorley's career. Brashear sits 15th on the NHL all-time PIM leader list with 2,634. His PIM total is third highest for any American-born player.

Did you know...

... Following his NHL playing career, former Flyers enforcer Donald Brashear briefly tried his hands at MMA. He won his 1st fight by TKO after just 21 seconds!

... Cuba Gooding jr, in the movie Men of Honor, portrayed former Flyers Donald Brashear's great-uncle Carl Brashear, the first African-American certified as a master diver in the US Navy.

Oddly enough...

87... During the 1986-87 NHL season, the Flyers led all teams with 205 fighting majors. It's the second-highest season total in NHL history.

87... Flyers goalie Pelle Lindbergh had 87 wins for the Flyers during his brief career. Lindbergh won his last NHL game prior to his death, a 6-2 victory over the Chicago Black Hawks on November 6th, 1985.

87... The Eagles have twice combined with an opponent to score a team-record 87 points in a single game. Both were with the Washington Redskins. The Eagles won both times, 59-28 on 11/15/10 in Washington, and 45-42 on 9/28/47 in Philly.

88

Eric Lindros – Flyers/C (1993-00) Simply put, Eric Lindros was a game changer. He redefined the role of the power forward. He was a dominating physical presence with a scorers touch. Lindros was the 4th fastest in NHL history to score 300 points, 4th fastest to score 400, 5th fastest to score 500, and 6th fastest to score 600 points. Lindros was a 7-time NHL All Star and won the Hart Memorial Trophy in 1995. Lindros had concussion issues that eventually forced him to retire. Yes, the Flyers gave up a ton to get him (Peter Forsberg, etc) and yes, it's disappointing Lindros couldn't bring us a Cup. Yes, he had his issues with the GM. Yes, our hearts were ripped out when Scott Stevens cruised the blueline and laid a vicious high hit on Lindros that left him crumpled on the ice. But for all the what-could-have-been's, it's tough to argue he was one of the very best to ever wear the orange and black. Lindros was named one of the greatest 100 players in NHL history, was inducted into the Hockey Hall of Fame in 2016. The Flyers retired his #88 in 2018.

Keith Jackson – Eagles/TE (1988-91) Keith Jackson played his first four pro seasons with the Birds after they drafted him 13th overall in the 1988 NFL Draft. Jackson was a Pro Bowler and a 1st Team All-Pro for each of his first three seasons. Jackson was the NFC Rookie of the Year in 1988. Jackson held Eagles franchise rookie record for receiving yards for 20 years until DeSean Jackson broke it in 2008.

John Spagnola – Eagles/TE (1979-87) John Spagnola spent nine seasons as an Eagles TE. In 1984, Spagnola was the Eagles offensive MVP. He was a Pro Bowl alternate in 1984, and 1985. In 1985 Spagnola and Mike Quick combined for 135 receptions and 2,019 receiving yards. This set a new team record for recs and yds by an Eagles duo (McDonald/Brown).

Did you know...

... Flyers Hall of Famer Eric Lindros was the 1st Flyer to score on multiple penalty shots when he scored his 2nd career penalty shot on December 26th, 1992 vs Washington Capitals.

... Flyers great Eric Lindros had a team-record 14 shots on goal on March 19th, 1996. Lindros finished the game with zero goals and two assists in a 4-1 Flyers win over the New York Islanders.

... Eagles long snapper/TE Mike Bartrum had 11 career catches at tight end. 6 were for touchdowns. It's the second highest TD/catch percentage in NFL history.

... Eagles TE Keith Jackson broke the Eagles rookie record for receptions in a season with 81 in 1988. The record stands 30 years later.

Even up...

88... Eagles kicker Cody Parkey holds the Eagles team rookie-record for FG pct. kicking 32 of 36 FGs for 88.9 pct. in 2014.

89

Calvin Williams – Eagles/WR (1990-96) Calvin Williams was drafted by the Eagles in the 5th round of the 1990 NFL Draft. The Birds drafted 2 other receivers ahead of Williams (Mike Bellamy, Fred Barnett). Williams won the starting spot and set a new Eagles rookie TD reception mark with nine. Williams led the Birds in TD receptions in 1990, '92, and '93. Williams is 8th all-time on the Eagles TD receptions list with 34, 15th in receptions with 295, and 12th in receiving yards with 3,840.

Chad Lewis – Eagles/TE (1997-98, 2000-05) Chad Lewis was a three-time Pro Bowler and an All Pro in 2000. In the 2004 playoffs, Lewis had two TD catches in the NFC Championship game against the Atlanta Falcons, including the game winner. During the second catch, Lewis suffered a Lisfranc foot injury that kept him out of Super Bowl XXXIX. Lewis ranks 34th on Eagles all-time receiving yards list with 2,349, 24th in receptions with 228, and 17th in receiving TDs with 23.

Did you know...

... Eagle WR Calvin Williams played high school basketball at Dunbar HS with NBA star Muggsy Bogues.

Oddly enough...

89... During the 1988-89 NHL season, the Flyers led all teams with 188 fighting majors. It's the third highest season total in NHL history.

89... Flyers Hall of Famer Bobby Clarke holds the team record for assists in a season with 89. Clarkie notched 89 assists in back-to-back seasons (1974-75 and 1975-76).

89... On September 27th, 2015, Eagles Darren Sproles had an 89-yard punt return for a TD vs New York Jets. It's the 2nd longest in team history (Damaris Johnson 98yds).

90

Corey Simon – Eagles/DT (2000-04) Corey Simon was selected 6th overall by the Eagles in the 2000 NFL Draft. He played five seasons on the Birds' D-line. Simon ranks 14th on the Eagles' career sacks list with 32. His 8 career forced fumbles ranks him 11th on the Eagles' all-time list. Simon was named to the 2000 NFL All-Rookie Team. In 2003, he was named to the Pro Bowl team.

Did you know...

... Eagles Corey Simon had a team rookie-record 9.5 sacks in 2000.

Even up...

90... Eagles Brian Westbrook had 90 receptions in 2007. Not only did that break the team record, but its more receptions than any Eagles WR ever had in a single season, and Westbrook did it out of the backfield.

90... Phillies relief pitcher Kent Tekulve appeared in a team-record 90 games for the Phillies in 1987.

91

Fletcher Cox – Eagles/DE-DT (2012-present) Fletcher Cox is a dominating defensive lineman that was selected 12th overall by the Eagles in the 2012 NFL Draft. Cox was selected for the 2015, 2016, 2017, and 2018 Pro Bowl team. Cox was a 1st Team All Pro for 2018 and a three-time 2nd Team All Pro (2014, 2015, 2017). He was named to the PFWA All Rookie Team in 2012. On September 7th, 2014, Cox recovered a fumble and ran 17 yards for a TD vs. Jacksonville Jaguars. On September 10th, 2017 Cox recovered a Kirk Cousins fumble and returned it 20 yards for a TD vs Washington Redskins. Both of Coxs' fumble recovery TDs were in season openers, and were the last score of the game. Cox was a member of the Eagles' Super Bowl LII championship team.

Andy Harmon – Eagles/DE-DT (1991-97) Andy Harmon was a defensive end who was converted into a defensive tackle in his second season with the Eagles. Though considered undersized for a defensive tackle, Harmon's speed enabled him to amass 39.5 career sacks, the most all-time for an Eagles DT, and 6th overall. His 11.5 sacks in 1993 are the most in a season for an Eagles DT. His 7 career forced fumbles ranks 13th on the Eagles list. Harmon was named to the 1995 Pro Bowl.

Did you know...

... In the movie Star Wars: The Force Awakens, an alien named Teedo speaks the words "Celek" and "Fletcher." In the movie Rogue One: A Star Wars Story, the Eagles fight song "Fly Eagles Fly" was used as a Jedha City chant. The sound engineer David Acord is a huge Eagles fan.

Oddly enough...

91... Eagles kicker Paul McFadden kicked 91 FGs during his Eagles career, good for 2nd best in team history (David Akers 294).

91... On November 27th, 1994, Eagles RB Herschel Walker had a team-record 91-yard rushing play vs Atlanta Falcons.

91... On December 3rd, 1989 Eagles QB/P Randall Cunningham kicked a team-record 91-yard punt vs New York Giants. It's the 4th longest in NFL history.

92

Reggie White – Eagles/DE (1985-92) The greatest Defensive End of all time! The Minister of Defense was selected 4th overall in the 1984 NFL Supplemental Draft after playing two seasons in the USFL. White was a Pro Bowler 13 times in his 15 NFL seasons (7 with the Eagles), only missing his first and last seasons in the league. He was a six-time 1st Team All Pro as an Eagle. During his time with the Birds, White was a two-time NFL Defensive Player of the Year, and a three-time NFC Defensive Player of the Year. He was also a two-time sack leader. The Minister of Defense is the Eagles all-time sack leader with 124, and his 198 career NFL sacks ranks 2nd all-time (Bruce Smith). White was named to the NFL 1980's All-Decade Team, 1990's All-Decade Team, and the NFL's 75th Anniversary Team. He is a member of the Eagles Hall of Fame and his #92 was retired. White entered the Pro Football Hall of Fame in 2006. White passed away in 2004 at the age of 43.

Did you know...

... In a shortened NFL season in 1987 Reggie White amassed 21 sacks in the 12-game season. He is the only NFL player is history to hit the 20-sack mark in just 12 games.

... Reggie White had a team-record 38 multi-sack games for the Eagles.

Even up...

92... Eagles Super Bowl LII MVP QB Nick Foles owns the team's best career QB rating with a 92.7 rating.

92... The Eagles scored a TD in 92 consecutive games from October 2nd, 1977 thru October 16th, 1983. The longest streak in team history.

93

Jakub Voracek – Flyers/RW (2011-present) Jake "scoracek" Voracek has been a leader on the Flyers since his arrival (along with draft pick used on Sean Couturier) in the trade that sent Jeff Carter to Columbus. On December 22nd, 2014, Voracek beat Ondrej Pavelec just ten seconds into overtime vs. Winnepeg Jets, becoming the second fastest to score an overtime goal in team history (Simon Gagne 7 sec). Voracek was named to the 2015 NHL All Star team for the game played in Columbus, where Voracek's career began. Playing in front of his former fans, Voracek tied NHL All Star single game points record with 6. Voracek finished 4th in the league in scoring and 2nd in assists for the 2014-15 season. He won the Bobby Clarke Trophy in 2013 and 2015, the Gene Hart Memorial Trophy in 2015, the Pelle Lindbergh Memorial Trophy in 2013, and the Yanick Dupre Memorial Class Guy Award in 2014.

Jevon Kearse – Eagles/DE (2004-07) Jevon Kearse spent 4 seasons with the Birds and was a defensive driving force on their Super Bowl XXXIX team that lost to the New England Patriots. The Freak was so named due to the unusual combination of an 86-inch wingspan, a 48-inch vertical leap, and 4.43 speed in the forty. Though Kearse played just 45 games for the Birds, his 22 sacks is 22nd all-time for the Eagles, and his 6 forced fumbles ranks 21st.

Did you know...

... Flyers Jake Voracek assisted on former Flyer RJ Umberger's goal that gave the Columbus Blue Jackets their first playoff goal in franchise history.

... Eagles DE Jason Babin tied a team-record with 3 three-sack games during the 2011 season (Reggie White 1986).

... The 1993 Phillies team that went to the World Series held 1st place for 161 out of 162 games during the regular season.

Oddly enough...

93... On October 23rd, 1993, the Phillies lost the 1993 World Series to the Toronto Blue Jays when Joe Carter hit a walk-off 3-run homer off Mitch Williams to win the series 4 games to 2.

93... On October 13th, 1993 Phillies pitcher Curt Schilling was named MVP of the 1993 NLCS.

94

Ndukwe Dike "N.D." Kalu – Eagles/DE (1997, 2001-05) "N.D." Kalu is of Nigerian descent but was born in Baltimore, Maryland. Kalu had a career-high 8 sacks in 2002. His 18.5 career sacks with the Birds ranks 26th on the Eagles all-time list. Kalu had a pick six vs Washington Redskins on October 5th, 2003 in an Eagles 27-25 victory. Kalu missed the entire 2004 season due to a torn ACL, missing Super Bowl XXXIX.

Did you know...

... Phillies Danny Jackson was third in the NL in wins with a 14-6 record before the season-ending 1994 baseball strike.

Even up...

94... Phillies legend Steve Carlton was inducted into the Baseball Hall of Fame in 1994.

94... Major League Baseball had its longest work-stoppage during the 1994 season. The season ground to a halt on August 12th, 1994. The Phillies were 54-61 in 115 games. Subsequently, 948 games were cancelled as well as the playoffs. It was the 1st season in 90 years to not have a World Series. Played resumed on April 2nd, 1995, with a 144-game schedule after a stoppage of 232 days.

95

William Fuller – Eagles/DE (1994-96) William Fuller was an outstanding pass rushing defensive end. Fuller, coming out of college, played two seasons with the Philadelphia Stars of the USFL, winning two championships. He spent 8 seasons in Houston before coming to the Eagles as a free agent in 1994. Fuller had a sack in 7 consecutive games for the Eagles his first season here, and was named to the Pro Bowl team and was 2nd Team UPI All Pro. Fuller was a Pro Bowler in each of his three seasons with the Birds, and was twice UPI 1st Team All Pro. Fuller had 35.5 sacks for the Eagles in just 46 games, 9th most in Eagles history.

John Bunting – Eagles/LB (1972-82) John Bunting was a blue-collar warrior who played eleven seasons for the Birds and played in Super Bowl XV. Bunting was not the most physically gifted LB, but he was a student of the game and played his heart out every snap. Bunting once played 62 consecutive games for the birds. Bunting once hit Tony Dorsett so hard he knocked the ball loose and broke a few of Dorsett's ribs. Bunting finished his career with the Philadelphia Stars of the USFL playing the 1983 and 1984 season with them.

Mychal Kendricks – Eagles/LB (2012-Present) Mychal Kendricks was a very versatile linebacker during his six seasons with the Eagles. His 14 career sacks currently puts him 29th in team history. His 338 tackles ranks 15th, 6 forced fumbles ranks 21st, and 27 passes defended ranks 16th. Kendricks was a member of the Eagles Super Bowl LII championship team.

Oddly enough...

95... On December 2nd, 1990, Eagles WR Fred Barnett scored a 95-yard TD vs Buffalo Bills. It's the longest rookie receiving TD in team history.

95... The Sixers had a team-record 95 2nd half points in a 160-122 victory over the Seattle Supersonics on December 20th, 1967.

95... Phillies legends Mike Schmidt and Richie Ashburn were both inducted into the baseball Hall of Fame in 1995.

96

Clyde Simmons – Eagles/DE (1986-93) Clyde Simmons was a dominant defensive end who spent 8 seasons with the Birds and was part of their tremendous Gang Green defense. Simmons was a three-time Pro Bowler, two-time 1st Team All Pro, and three-time NFC Defensive Player of the Week. Simmons led the NFL is sacks in 1992 with 19. His 76.0 career sacks with the Eagles puts him 3rd on their all-time list. He is 5th in tackles with 720, and 6th in forced fumbles with 12. Simmons scored four non-offensive TDs during his Eagles career. He was named to the Eagles 75th Anniversary Team. Simmons entered the Eagles Hall of Fame in 2018.

Bennie Logan – Eagles/DT (2013-16) Bennie Logan spent four seasons with the Eagles. Logan was more of a run stopper than a pass rusher. Logan had 5.5 sacks during his stint with the Birds, but shined against the run where he was a top ten run stuffer two years in a row. Logan declined the Eagles contract offer and left after the 2016 season via free agency.

Derek Barnett – Eagles/DE (2017-Present) Derek Barnett was taken with the 14th overall pick in the 2017 NFL Draft. Barnett was named to the PFWA All Rookie Team for 2017. On Christmas Day 12/25/2017 vs Oakland Raiders Barnett recovered a fumble and ran 23 yards for his first career TD as time expired. Barnett also recovered the fumble on the infamous

Brandon Graham strip of Tom Brady in the 4th quarter of Super Bowl LII vs New England Patriots, helping the Eagles to their franchise's first Super Bowl Championship.

Did you know...

... On October 5th, 1996 the Flyers lost 3-1 to the Florida Panthers in the Flyers debut regular season game at the Core States Center (Wells Fargo Center).

... Flyers Dainus Zubrus scored the 1st Flyers goal at the newly opened Core States Center on 10/5/96, a 3-1 loss to the Florida Panthers. Shjon Podein and Chris Therien assisted on the goal at 4:04 of the 1st period.

... The 1st Flyers penalty at the Core States Center was, of course, a fighting major. Flyers Dan Kordic dropped the gloves with Florida Panthers Paul Laus at 8:11 of the 1st period in the Flyers 1st-ever game at their new facility on 10/5/1996.

... Flyers Legion of Doom winger John LeClair scored the first-ever goal at the Core States Center in the 1st period of the World Cup of Hockey tournament game between the US and Canada on August 31st, 1996. The US won 5-3.

Even up...

96... On July 9th, 1996, the Phillies hosted their 3rd MLB All Star Game.

97

Jeremy Roenick – Flyers/C (2001-04) Jeremy Roenick was a huge free agent signing for the Flyers in the summer of 2001. He scored his 1,000th NHL point on January 30th 2002 vs Ottawa Senators. The following season, on November 16th, 2002, Roenick played his 1,000th NHL game. Roenick led the Flyers in points two of his three seasons in the orange and black, and could have led them a third time had it not been for a devastating jaw injury suffered off a slap shot by New York Ranger defenseman Boris Mironov on February 12th, 2004. The blast shattered JR's jaw in 19 pieces. Initially, there was thought to be nerve damage and that the damage was career-threatening. It turned out there was no nerve damage, and Roenick returned two weeks before the playoffs. Roenick played in three consecutive NHL All Star games while with the Flyers. During the 2004 NHL All Star Skills Competition, Roenick tied the NHL record going 4 for 4 in the shooting accuracy contest. JR won the Bobby Clarke Trophy and the Yanick Dupre Memorial Class Guy Award in 2002.

Rhett Hall – Eagles/DT-DE (1995-98) Rhett Hall was a defensive lineman who followed Coach Ray Rhoads from the Super Bowl-winning San Francisco 49ers to the Eagles for the 1995 NFL season. However, during training camp Hall developed shortness of breath. He was found to have a pulmonary embolism and blood clots. Hall missed most of the season, returning for game 15. Hall played very well over the next two seasons.

On September 30th, 1996 Hall picked up a Dallas Cowboy fumble and ran 32 yards for the only TD of his career. Hall had 77 tackles and 13.5 sacks before knee injuries kept him to just two games in 1998, leading to his retirement. Hall was the recipient of the Ed Block Courage Award in 1997.

Darwin Walker – Eagles/DT (2000-06) Darwin Walker was a starting defensive tackle for the Eagles teams that went to four-consecutive NFC Championship games and Super Bowl XXXIX. Walker played 87 games for the Birds. His 27.5 sacks ranks 19th on the Eagles all-time list. His 6 forced fumbles ranks 21st, and 14 passes defended ranks 34th.

Did you know...

... Former Flyer Jeremy Roenick's middle name is Shaffer.

... On November 10th, 2007 Jeremy Roenick became just the 3rd American-born NHLer to score his 500th goal (Joe Mullen, Mike Modano). A few weeks later Roenick passed Mullen for 2nd place all-time.

... Former Flyers Jeremy Roenick and Tony Amonte were not only linemates with the Flyers and the Chicago Black Hawks, they were linemates in HS at Thayer Academy.

... Former Flyer Jeremy Roenick was the 1st NHLer to ever wear the #97 (Phoenix Coyotes 1997-98)

98

Connor Barwin – Eagles/LB (2013-16) Connor Barwin started all 64 games of his four-year Eagles career. On November 3rd, 2013 Barwin nabbed his first and only career interception in a 49-20 Eagle victory over the Oakland Raiders. Two weeks later Barwin had 12 tackles against the Washington Redskins. For the 2014 season, Barwin was the NFC Player of the Month for November, led the NFC in sacks with 14.5, was a Pro Bowler and 2nd Team All Pro.   Barwin is 15th on the Eagles all-time sack list with 31.5, 18th in passes defended with 26, and 21st in forced fumbles with 6.

Greg Brown – Eagles/DT-DE (1981-86) Greg Brown played parts of six seasons with the Birds and was a three-year starter. His 50.5 career sacks ranks 5th best on Eagles all-time list. On September 27th, 1981 Brown had a 7-yard fumble recovery for a TD in a 36-13 win over the Washington Redskins. On December 26th, 1982 Brown recovered a fumble in the endzone for his second career fumble recovery touchdown in a 24-20 victory over the Dallas Cowboys.

Mike Patterson – Eagles/DT (2005-12) Mike Patterson was a first round selection (31st overall) in the 2005 NFL Draft following the team's Super Bowl XXXIX loss. Prior to the 2011 season, after collapsing and suffering a seizure during training camp, Patterson was diagnosed with a cerebral arteriovenous malformation. He played 15 games that season and had brain surgery in January 2012. Patterson played 115 games for the Birds. His 16.5 sacks ranks 27th on the Eagles all-time list. His 255 tackles ranks 25th.

Did you know...

... On September 24th, 2006, Eagles DT Mike Patterson recovered a San Francisco 49ers fumble at the two-yard line and ran 98 yards for a touchdown. It's the longest fumble recovery in team history.

Even up...

98... On December 2nd, 2012, vs Dallas Cowboys, Eagles Damaris Johnson returned a punt 98-yards for a TD. It's the longest punt return in team history.

98... Phillies slugger Greg Luzinski joined the Phillies Wall of Fame in 1998.

99

Jerome Brown – Eagles/DT (1987-91) Jerome Brown was a dominating defensive lineman and part of the Eagles infamous Gang Green. He was drafted 9th overall in the 1987 NFL Draft. Brown was selected to the 1987 NFL All-Rookie Team. Brown was a two-time NFC Defensive Player of the Week, two-time Pro Bowler, and two-time 1st Team All Pro. Brown's 29.5 career sacks is 18th on the Eagles all-time list. Brown was named to the Eagles 75th Anniversary Team, and the Eagles Hall of Fame in 1996. Jerome Brown died in a car crash on June 25th, 1992 in Brooksville, Florida at the age of 27. The Eagles retired Jerome Brown's #99 prior to the season opener in 1992.

Did you know...

... The 2017 Philadelphia Eagles won Super Bowl LII on what would have been Jerome Brown's 53rd birthday.

Oddly enough...

99... Tug McGraw entered the Phillies Wall of Fame in 1999.

99... Phillies C Mike Leiberthal won his only Gold Glove in 1999.

99... Three Phillies have worn the #99 in team history (So Taguchi 2008, Turk Wendell 2001, Mitch Williams 1993).

100

Wilt Chamberlain on March 2, 1962 in Hershey Pennsylvania, as a member of the Philadelphia Warriors scored his all-time record 100 points in the game. The Warriors won the game 169-147. The combined 316 points is also an NBA record. Chamberlain set 6 records that night. The Big Dipper had his incredible performance in front of a very meager 4,124 attendees, and no broadcast tape.

Phillies Hot Corner

PHILADELPHIA PHILLIES

Number of seasons played – 136 (most of any professional sports team in North America) 1883- to current (*through 2018 season)

Record – 9744 wins – 10,919 losses .472 winning percentage*

Playoff appearances – 14

World Series appearances – 7 (1916, 1950, 1980, 1983, 1993, 2008, 2009)

World Series Championships – 2 (1980, 2008)

Phillies in Baseball Hall of Fame

(year inducted)

Grover C. Alexander P (1938)	Chuck Klein RF (1980)
Ed Delahanty LF (1945)	Steve Carlton P (1994)
Harry Wright Executive (1953)	Mike Schmidt 3B (1995)
Billy Hamilton OF (1961)	Richie Ashburn CF (1995)
Dave Bancroft SS (1971)	Jim Bunning P (1996)
Sam Thompson RF (1974)	Jim Thome OF/1B (2018)
Robin Roberts P (1976)	Roy Halladay P (2019)

Retired Phillies jersey numbers

P – Chuck Klein	#14 – Jim Bunning
HK – Harry Kalas	#20 – Mike Schmidt
P – Grover Cleveland Alexander	#32 – Steve Carlton
#1 – Richie Ashburn	#36 – Robin Roberts

Phillies Wall of Fame

Robin Roberts 1978

Richie Ashburn 1979

Chuck Klein 1980

Grover C. Alexander 1981

Del Ennis 1982

Jim Bunning 1984

Ed Delahanty 1985

Cy Williams 1986

Granny Hamner 1987

Paul Owens 1988

Steve Carlton 1989

Mike Schmidt 1990

By Saam 1990

Larry Bowa 1991

Chris Short 1992

Curt Simmons 1993

Dick Allen 1994

Willie Jones 1995

Sam Thompson 1996

Johnny Callison 1997

Greg Luzinski 1998

Tug McGraw 1999

Gavvy Cravat 2000

Garry Maddox 2001

Harry Kalas 2002

Tony Taylor 2002

Sherry Magee 2003

Billy Hamilton 2004

Bob Boone 2005

Dallas Green 2006

John Vukovich 2007

Juan Samuel 2008

Harry Kalas 2009

Darren Daulton 2010

John Kruk 2011

Mike Lieberthal 2012

Curt Schilling 2013

Charlie Manuel 2014

Pat Burrell 2015

Jim Thome 2016

Pat Gillick 2018

Roy Halladay 2018

ALL-TIME LEADERS

Hitting

WAR – Mike Schmidt, 106.5

Games played – Mike Schmidt, 2,404

ABs – Jimmy Rollins, 8,628

HRs – Mike Schmidt, 548

RBIs – Mike Schmidt, 1,595

BBs – Mike Schmidt, 1,507

HBP – Chase Utley, 173

SB% - Chase Utley, 88.75%

Pitching

Wins – Steve Carlton, 241

Starts – Steve Carlton, 499

Appearances – Robin Roberts, 529

Innings pitched – Robin Roberts, 3,739.1

Strikeouts – Steve Carlton, 3,031

Saves – Jonathan Papelbon, 123

Did you know...

... The Phillies have been to the World Series 7 times in 136 years. Three of those appearances came within a 14-year period. 33 years till 1st, 35 years till the next, 30 years till next which began 3 in 14 years, then a 15-year wait before 2 in a row for the first time in team history.

... Phillies shortstop Jimmy Rollins had a MLB-record 716 ABs in 2007.

... Phillies Hall of Famer Steve Carlton holds the MLB record for pick-offs with 144.

... Phillies Jamie Moyer became the oldest pitcher to win a game in MLB history on May 16th, 2012.

... The Phillies and the Athletics have made 12 trades during their team's histories. Only two were while both were in Philly.

... 54 different pitchers have started a season opener for the Phillies since 1908.

Start your engines... Most season opening starts per position...

C Mike Leiberthal 10,

1B Ryan Howard 10,

2B Chase Utley 8,

3B Mike Schmidt 16,

SS Jimmy Rollins 14,

RF Johnny Callison 9,

CF Richie Ashburn 10,

LF Greg Luzinski 9,

SP Lefty Steve Carlton 14,

SP Righty Robin Roberts 12.

Where there's smoke... The Phillies have had 3 300+ strikeout seasons by their pitchers in team history. Curt Schilling did it in back-to-back seasons racking up a team-record 319 Kos in 1997 and followed that up with a team-3rd best 300 in 1998. Hall of Famer Steve Carlton had a team-2nd best 310 in 1972.

Did you know...

... The Robert Redford movie "The Natural" is based on the life of Phillies 1B Eddie Waitkus.

... The Phillies have had two players in their history record an unassisted triple play. Mickey Morandini had the 9th triple play in the modern era in 1992, and Eric Bruntlett had the 15th in 2009. Both triple plays were off the bats of Jeffs (Jeff King 1992, Jeff Francoeur 2009).

... Phillies pitcher Jake Thompson had 4 strikeouts in the 2nd inning vs Colorado Rockies on 8/12/16. He was the 1st Phillies pitcher to ever accomplish the feat. Thompson was just in his 6th MLB inning and second MLB game.

... The Phils have struck out four times in an inning twice in their history. 4/17/65 (Don Drysdale) and 6/21/2008 (Scot Shields).

... The Phillies have hosted 3 All Star games, 1952, 1976, and 1996. The Philadelphia Athletics were the first to host a MLB All Star game in Philly, hosting in 1943.

... The Phillies and the Philadelphia Athletics both hosted a MLB All Star game on July 13th. The A's in 1943, and the Phils in 1976.

Eagles Eyrie

PHILADELPHIA EAGLES

Number of seasons played – 86

Record – 577-601-26

Playoff appearances – 39

Championships – 4 (NFL Championship 1948, 1949, 1960) Super Bowl 2018 Super Bowl LII

Eagles in Pro Football Hall of Fame (year inducted)

Chuck Bednarik
C/LB (1967)

Bert Bell Owner
(1963)

Bill Hewitt E (1971)

Sonny Jurgensen
QB (1983)

Earl "Greasy"
Neale   HC (1969)

Pete Pihos E (1970)

Norm Van Brocklin
QB (1971)

Steve Van Buren
HB (1965)

Reggie White DE
(2006)

Bob Brown T
(2004)

Ollie Matson HB
(1972)

Tommy McDonald
WR (1998)

Jim Ringo C (1981)

Alex Wojciechowicz
C (1968)

Brian Dawkins   S
(2018)

Terrell Owens WR
(2018)

Retired Eagles Jersey Numbers

#5 - Donovan McNabb

#15 - Steve Van Buren

#20 - Brian Dawkins

#40 - Tom Brookshier

#44 - Pete Retzlaff

#60 - Chuck Bednarik

#70 - Al Wistert

#92 - Reggie White

#99 - Jerome Brown

Eagles Hall of Fame

Chuck Bednarik 1987

Harold Carmichael 1987

Bill Hewitt 1987

Sonny Jurgensen 1987

Wilbert Montgomery 1987

Pete Pihos 1987

Norm Van Brocklin 1987

Steve Van Buren 1987

Ollie Matson 1987

Jim Ringo 1987

Alex Wojciechowicz 1987

Bill Bergey 1988

Tommy McDonald 1988

Tom Brookshier 1989

Pete Retzlaff 1989

Tim Brown 1990

Jerry Sisemore 1991

Stan Walters 1991

Ron Jaworski 1992

Bill Bradley 1993

Mike Quick 1995

Jerome Brown 1996

Bob Brown 2004

Reggie White 2005

Randall Cunningham 2009

Al Wistert 2009

Eric Allen 2011

Brian Dawkins 2012

Maxie Baughan 2015

Jeremiah Trotter 2016

Troy Vincent 2012

Brian Westbrook 2015

Seth Joyner 2018

Donovan McNabb 2013

Clyde Simmons 2018

Bert Bell Owner 1987

Otho Davis Head Trainer 1999

Earl "Greasy" Neale Head Coach 1987

Jim Johnson defensive coordinator 2011

Dick Vermeil Head Coach 1994

Leo Carlin executive 2012

Jim Gallagher Executive 1995

Merrill Reese Radio Broadcaster 2016

1948, 1949 NFL Championship Teams 1999

ALL-TIME LEADERS

Offensive

       Rushing – LeSean McCoy, 6,792 yds

       Passing – Donovan McNabb, 32,837 yds

       Receptions – Harold Carmichael, 589

       Receiving yards – Harold Carmichael, 8,978

Scoring – David Akers, 1,323 pts

Games Played – David Akers, 188

Touchdowns – Harold Carmichael, 79

TD passes – Donovan McNabb, 216

Completions – Donovan McNabb, 2,801

Rushing TDs – Steve Van Buren, 69

Defensive

Interceptions – Brian Dawkins, 34

Sacks – Reggie White, 124.0

Tackles – Andre Waters, 910

Forced Fumbles – Brian Dawkins, 32

Fumble Recovery TDs – Seth Joyner, 3

Pick 6's – Eric Allen, 5

NFL RECORDS HELD BY AN EAGLE

Most Touchdown Passes, Game - 7

Nick Foles (11/3/2013 at Raiders)

Adrian Burk (10/17/1954 at Redskins);   tied with 6 others

Longest TD Pass – 99 yards

Ron Jaworski to Mike Quick, (11/10/1985 vs. Falcons) (OT);

Most Interception Returns for TDs, Season – 4

Eric Allen, 1993; tied with two others

Most Interceptions, Game – 4

Russ Craft (9/24/1950 at Cardinals); tied with 17 others

Most Kickoff Return TDs, Game - 2

Timmy Brown (11/6/1966 vs. Cowboys), 93, 90 yards;

tied with 7 others

Most 50-Plus-Yard Touchdowns, Season - 8

DeSean Jackson (2009); tied with 2 others

Pick 6's in a season – 4 Eric Allen 1993

Did you know...

... In the 2000 season opener, Sept. 3rd, the Eagles and Cowboys played in "the pickle-juice" game. The temp was 109 degrees Fahrenheit at kick off and the temperature rose throughout the game. The Eagles training staff had players drinking juice from dill pickle jars to retain body moisture and fight dehydration. It worked. A number of Cowboys were sidelined from the oppressive Texas heat but no Eagles were. The eagles won 44-14.

Did you know...

... The Eagles have the only left-facing logo in the NFL. The Eagle feathers form the letter "E" for Eagles.

... In 1943, finding it difficult to field a complete team due to the war in Europe, the Eagles and Pittsburgh Steelers merged for the season and called themselves the Steagles. It was the Eagles first winning season going 5-4-1.

... Prior to coaching the Eagles, Earl "Greasy" Neale was an outfielder for the Cincinnati Reds and Philadelphia Phillies from 1918-1922, debuting with Cincinnati on April 12th, 1916. Neale played for the Phillies during the 1921 season.

... The Eagles have selected five 1st round picks from USC. No other college has provided the Eagles with more than three 1st round selections. The 1st round picks from USC are Nelson Agholor 2015, Mike Patterson 2005, Charle Young 1973, Tim Rossovich 1968, and Leo Riggs 1946.

... Eagles kicker David Akers made a team-record 173 consecutive PATs from 2004-2009.

... Eagles Super Bowl LII MVP QB Nick Foles holds the team record for lowest INT pct in a single season with 0.63 in 2013. He threw just 2 INTs in 317 pass attempts.

Best of Eagles Wall of Famer - Defensive Coordinator Jim Johnson

From 2000-2007 the Johnson-led Eagles defense amassed 342 sacks, tied for 1st in NFL

In 2001, Johnson's defense became just the 4th team in NFL history to hold opponents to 21 pts or less in every game of a complete 16-game season.

Jim Johnson sent Eagles to the Pro Bowl 26 times: Brian Dawkins (7), Troy Vincent (5), Jeremiah Trotter (4), Hugh Douglas (3), Lito Sheppard (2), Trent Cole, Michael Lewis, Asante Samuel, Corey Simon, Bobby Taylor (1).

3 - # of current NFL Head Coaches that were assistants under Jim Johnson (John Harbaugh, Ron Rivera, Sean McDermott)

On February 4th, 2018 the Eagles defeated the New England Patriots to win Super Bowl LII, 41-33 to capture their first Super Bowl Championship and becoming the 20th NFL team to win it. (12 teams still have not won a Super Bowl, and 4 teams have zero appearances).

Here are some of the NFL records re-written during the game...

Most combined total yards in a Super Bowl ... 1,151 yards

Most passing yards in a postseason game – 505, Tom Brady

Most points scored by the losing team in a Super Bowl – 33, New England Patriots

Most total passing yards in a Super Bowl – 874

First player to throw and catch a TD in the same Super Bowl – Nick Foles

First QB to catch a touchdown pass in the Super Bowl – Nick Foles

Longest FG by a rookie in a Super Bowl – 46 yards, Jake Elliott

Fewest punts returned (both teams) – 0

Flyers Face Off Circle

PHILADELPHIA FLYERS

Number of seasons played – 50

Record – 1976-1371-457-160 (4,569 points)

Playoff appearances – 39

Championships – 2

Flyers in Hockey Hall of Fame (year inducted)

Bernie Parent (1984)   Mark Recchi (2017)

Bobby Clarke (1987)   Ed Snider   Builder (1988)

Bill Barber (1990)   Keith Allen   Builder (1992)

Mark Howe (2011)   Fred Shero Builder (2013)

Eric Lindros (2016)

Other former Flyers elected to the Hockey Hall of Fame...

Allan Stanley (1981)

Darryl Sittler (1989)

Dale Hawerchuk (2001)

Paul Coffey (2004)

Adam Oates (2012)

Peter Forsberg (2014)

Chris Pronger (2015)

Bud Poile   Builder (1990)

Roger Neilson Builder (2002)

Pat Quinn Builder (2016)

Flyers Retired Jersey Numbers

#1 Bernie Parent

#2 Mark Howe

#4 Barry Ashbee

#7 Bill Barber

#16 Bobby Clarke

#88 Eric Lindros

Flyers Hall of Fame

Bernie Parent (1988)

Bob Clarke (1988)

Bill Barber (1989)

Rick MacLeish (1990)

Barry Ashbee (1991)

Gary Dornhoefer (1991)

Reg Leach (1992)

Ed Van Impe (1993)

Tim Kerr (1994)

Joe Watson (1996)

Brian Propp (1999)

Mark Howe (2001)

Dave Poulin (2004)

Ron Hextall (2008)

Dave Schultz (2009)

John LeClair (2014)

Eric Lindros (2014)

Rod Brind'Amour
(2015)

Eric Desjardins
(2015)

Jimmy Watson
(2016)

Joe Scott (Exec)
(1993)

Keith Allen (Exec)
(1989)

Ed Snider (Owner)
(1989)

Fred Shero
(Coach) (1990)

Gene Hart
(Broadcaster)
(1992)

ALL-TIME LEADERS

Flyers 50-goal scorers

Rick MacLeish 50 1972-73

Reg Leach 61 1975-76

Bill Barber 50 1975-76

Reg Leach 50 1979-80

Tim Kerr 54 1983-84, 1984-85

58 1985-86, 1986-87

Mark Recchi 53 1992-93

John LeClair 51 1995-96, 1997-98

50 1996-97

100-Point Seasons

Bobby Clarke 104 1972-73, 116 1974-75, 119 1975-76

Rick MacLeish 100 1972-73

Bill Barber 112 1975-76

Mark Recchi 123 1992-93, 107 1993-94

Eric Lindros 115 1995-96

Claude Giroux 102 2017-18

All Time Leaders –

Games played – Bob Clarke, 1,144

Goals – Bill Barber, 420

Assists – Bobby Clarke, 852

Points – Bobby Clarke, 1,210

Plus/minus – Bobby Clarke, +506

PIMs – Rick Tocchet, 1,817

PP goals – Tim Kerr, 145

SH goals – Bobby Clarke, 32

GW goals – John LeClair, 61

Hat Tricks – Tim Kerr, 17

PPG avg. – Eric Lindros, 1.36

Games played (goalie) – Ron Hextall, 489

Wins – Ron Hextall, 240

Shutouts – Bernie Parent, 50

GAA – Roman Cechmanek, 1.96

Most goals in a season – Reg Leach, 61   1975-76

Most assists in a season – Bobby Clarke, 89 1974-75, 1975-76

Most goals in a season (plus playoffs) – Reg Leach, 80   1975-76

Most points in a season – Mark Recchi, 123   1992-93

Plus/minus – Mark Howe, +85 1992-93

PIMs – Dave Schultz, 475   1974-75

PP goals – Tim Kerr, 34   1985-86

SH goals – Brian Propp, 7 1984-85, Mark Howe, 7   1985-86,

Mike Richards, 7 2008-09

Save pct – Steve Mason .927 2014-15

GAA – Roman Cechmanek, 1.83   2002-03

Shutouts – Bernie Parent, 12   1973-74, 1974-75

NHL Records

PIMs by a goaltender in a single playoff year – Ron Hextall, 43 1986-87

PIMs in a playoff game - Dave Schultz, 42 PIMs 4/22/76

Goals in a playoff year – Reggie Leach, 19 1976 (Jari Kurri tied it in 1985)

Goals in a playoff game – Reggie Leach, 5 5/6/76 (tied w 4 others)

Most goals in a single period – Tim Kerr, 4 4/13/85 (tied w 12 others)

Overtime goals by a rookie in one season – Shayne Gostisbehere, 4 2015-2016

Points in NHL Debut – Al Hill, 5 2/14/77

Rookie Defenseman consecutive game scoring streak – Shayne Gostisbehere, 15 1/19/16 to 2/20/16

Points in a game for a defenseman – Tom Bladon, 8 on 12/11/77 (4 goals, 4 assists).   (Paul Coffey tied the record)

Highest single game plus/minus – Tom Bladon, +10 12/11/77 (his 8-pt night)

Flyers Captains – 18

Lou Angotti 1967-68

Ed Van Impe 1968-72

Bobby Clarke 1972-79, 1982-84

Mel Bridgeman 1979-81

Bill Barber 1981-82

Dave Poulin 1984-89

Ron Sutter 1989-91

Rick Tocchet 1991-92

Kevin Dineen 1993-94

Eric Lindros 1994-99

Eric Desjardins 1999-01

Keith Primeau 2001-05

Derrian Hatcher 2005-06

Peter Forsberg 2006-07

Jason Smith 2007-08

Mike Richards 2008-11

Chris Pronger 2011-12

Claude Giroux 2012-

Flyers Greatest Line Nicknames

Legion of Doom – Forward line with John LeClair, Eric Lindros, and Mikael Renberg. Teammate Jim Montgomery, regarding the line's size and physical dominance, said "It's like the Legion of Doom out there!"

Crazy 8's line – Mark Recchi (8), Brent Fedyk (18), and Eric Lindros (88). Right-handed Brent Fedyk played on the left side, while left-handed Mark Recchi, played on the right.

LCB line – Reg Leach, Bobby Clarke, and Bill Barber formed one of the best lines in Flyers history.

The French Line – French-Canadian line with Jean-Guy Gendron, Andre Lacroix, and Simon Nolet.

The Dan Line – 4th line tough guys Dan Kordic, Dan Lacroix, and Scott Daniels.

The Redemption Line – Ville Leino, Scott Hartnell, and Danny Briere. Potent playoff line for Flyers.

Deuces Wild – Simon Gagne (12), Peter Forsberg (21) and Mike Knuble (22).

Hi-Speed Line – Ron Flockhart, Ray Allison, and Brian Propp.

Ginger Line – top-scoring line all with ginger red hair, Captain Claude Giroux, Scott Hartnell, and Jake Voracek.

Sesame Street Line – Dave Schultz (Grouch), Don Saleski (Big Bird), and Orest Kindrachuk (Oscar).

The "G" Line – Jaromir Jagr, Scott Hartnell, Claude Giroux.

The Minnesota Line – Trent Klatt, Shjon Podein, and Joel Otto. Top shutdown line all hailing from Minnesota.

Blackhawk Down Line – Alexei Zhamnov, Jeremy Roenick, and Tony Amonte. All former Chicago Black Hawks.

Legion of Gloom – Dale Weise, Jori Lehtera, and Valtteri Filppula

Center City Line – Joffrey Lupul, Jeff Carter, and Scott Hartnell. All three lived in Center City Philly.

Honey Bees – Taylor Leier, Michael Raffl, and Scott Laughton (Black and yellow practice jerseys).

Did you know...

... NHL Hall of Fame goaltender Bernie Parent played professionally for two Philadelphia hockey franchises, the NHL's Philadelphia Flyers (two stints) and the WHA's Philadelphia Blazers (1972-73). Ironically, Parent played his junior hockey with the Niagara Falls Flyers (1963-64, 1964-65) and started his pro career in the minors with the Oklahoma City Blazers (1965-66, 1966-67).

... From 1963-1965, the goaltending tandem of Bernie Parent and Doug Favell manned the nets for their junior hockey team the Niagara Falls Flyers. From 1967 to 1971 they were the goaltending tandem for the Philadelphia Flyers. On May 5th, 1973 as part of a deal that eventually involved five players, Parent and Favell were traded for each other.

... The Flyers are 100-30-5 when Kate Smith sings God Bless America before a game. Kate Smith's version of God Bless America debuted with the Flyers on December 11th, 1969 vs Toronto Maple Leafs, a Flyers 6-3 win. Kate Smith sang in person for the first time at a Flyers game before their 1973 season home opener also vs Toronto Maple Leafs. The Flyers won 2-0.

... The Flyers very first penalty-free game was March 18th, 1979 vs St. Louis Blues. Flyers won 5-3.

... On April 12th, 1973, the Flyers won their 1st playoff series knocking off the Minnesota North Stars 4 games to 2.

Did you know...

... On March 14th, 1968, vs Los Angeles Kings, the Flyers skated to their 1st 0-0 scoreless tie.

... On June 6th, 1966, Keith Allen was named 1st head coach in Flyers team history.

... Claude Giroux (2008) is the only Flyer to ever wear #56. He wore it for two games before switching to #28.

... On Jan 11th, 1976, the Flyers hosted the Moscow Central Red Army ice hockey team as part of the Super Series tour. After a vicious first period hit by Flyer's defenseman Ed Van Impe on the Red Army's Valeri Kharlamov, the Soviet coach Konstantin Loktev pulled his team from the ice. It took Ed Snider threatening the Soviets with not getting paid to get them back on the ice. It's one of the iconic moments of the Broad Street Bullies. An irate Loktev called the Flyers play, "Animal Hockey." Ironically, the tournament slogan that was printed on the game tickets: "May We Live In Peace." The Flyers won the game 4-1 outshooting the Soviets 48-13 and were the only NHL team to beat the Red Army team during the Super Series of 1975-1976.

... In 1975, capitalizing on his unprecedented popularity in Philadelphia as "The Hammer," Dave Schultz released a 45 rpm record of the kitschy "Penalty Box."

Did you know...

... Seven players have (to date) been the only players to wear their number in Flyers history (minimum 60 games) #68 Jaromir Jagr, #76 Chris VandeVelde, #78 Pierre-Edouard Bellemare, #87 Donald Brashear, #88 Eric Lindros, #92 Rick Tocchet, and #97 Jeremy Roenick.

... The Flyers have had at least one future Hall of Famer on their roster every season since their inception in 1967-68 thru the 2006-07 season. Flyers star Claude Giroux joined the Flyers for the 2007-08 season. We'll just have to wait a while to see if the streak continues.

... The Flyers had 3 future Hall of Famers on their roster for each season from 1973-74 thru 1978-79 (Bernie Parent, Bobby Clarke, and Bill Barber). They had three future Hall of Famers during the 1982-83 season (Bill Barber, Bobby Clarke, and Darryl Sittler). The Flyers had a team-high 4 future Hall of Famers during the 1982-83 and 1983-84 seasons when Mark Howe joined the mix. The Flyers once again had 3 future Hall of Famers during the 1996-97 season with Eric Lindros, Paul Coffey, and Dale Hawerchuk.

... Of the six uniform numbers retired by the Flyers, only three (#1 Bernie Parent, #16 Bob Clarke, #88 Eric Lindros) were never worn again after them (#2 Mark Howe- ten others, #4 Barry Ashbee- 3 others, #7 Bill Barber- 3 others).

Sixers Net Effect

PHILADELPHIA SIXERS

Number of seasons played – 69   1963- present

(Syracuse Nationals from 1949-50 to 1962-63)

Record – 2806-2662   .513

Playoff appearances – 48

Conference Championships – 9

Championships – 3 (1 as Nationals)

Sixers in Basketball Hall of Fame (year inducted)

Dolph Schayes (1973)

Wilt Chamberlain (1979)

Hal Greer (1982)

Al Cervi (1985)

Billy Cunningham (1986)

Julius Erving (1993)

Moses Malone (2001)

Charles Barkley (2006)

Chet Walker (2012)

Dikembe Mutombo (2015)

Allen Iverson (2016)

George McGinnis (2017)

Jack Ramsey Head Coach (1992)

Alex Hannum Head Coach (1998)

Larry Brown Head Coach (2002)

Maurice Cheeks (2018)

Sixers Retired Jersey Numbers

#3 – Allen Iverson

#4 – Dolph Schayes

#6 – Julius Erving

#10 – Maurice Cheeks

#13 – Wilt Chamberlain

#15 – Hal Greer

#24 – Bobby Jones

#32 – Billy Cunningham

#34 – Charles Barkley

Dave Zinkoff – Public Address Announcer

ALL TIME TEAM LEADERS

Points – Hal Greer, 21,586

Minutes played – Hal Greer, 39,788

Rebounds – Dolph Schayes, 11,256

Assists – Maurice Cheeks, 6,212

Steals – Maurice Cheeks, 1,942

Blocks – Julius Erving, 1,293

3 pointers – Allen Iverson, 885

Did you know...

... The Sixers are the oldest franchise in the NBA.

... The Sixers have never had a player with a last name beginning with the letter Z. The Phillies have had 7, the Eagles have had 11, and the Flyers have had 12. Even the Philadelphia Warriors had one, Zeke Zawoluk 1953-55. The Sixers have also never had a Q, or U. None of the teams have had a X.

... The Sixers have had 12 players on their roster from Duke University, the most from any college (Alaa Abdelnaby, Elton Brand, Johnny Dawkins, Mike Gminski, David Henderson, Gerald Henderson, Art Heyman, Antonio Lang, Roshown McLeod, Jahlil Okafor, Shavlik Randolph, and Jim Spanarkle).

... Sixer Hall of Famer Hal Greer played 39,788 minutes for the Sixers during his career. That's 27 days, 15 hours, and 8 minutes. It's over 7 days more than Allen Iverson who is 2nd most.

... The Sixers scored a team-record 163 points vs the San Francisco Warriors (the team they replaced in Philly). The Sixers beat the Warriors 163-148 on March 10th, 1963.

... The 1972-73 Sixers team went 9-73, the worst record in NBA history.

... The 2013-2014 Sixers lost 26 games in a row from January 31st, 2014 thru March 27th, 2014. The Sixers 9-73 team of 1972-73 had their longest losing streak only reach 20 games.

... The 2017-18 Sixers won their last 16 games of the season, an NBA record for consecutive wins to end the season.

... The 2017-2018 Sixers postseason appearance was their 48th in team history, 3rd most ever in the NBA (Los Angeles Lakers – 60, Boston Celtics – 55).

... Sixer Larry Costello was the last NBA player to use the two-handed set shot.

... Sixers G Hal Greer once scored 19 points in one quarter of the 1967-68 NBA All-Star game. Greer played just 17 minutes, scored 21 points, and was named the game's MVP.

... The Sixers went from 10 wins in 2015-16 to 52 wins in 2017-18, the biggest two-year jump in NBA history.

Phifty Philly Phirsts

Phillies Phirsts

Phillies slugger Von Hayes was the 1st player in MLB history to hit two HRs in the 1st inning of a game when he pounded a leadoff HR off New York Mets starter Tom Gorman, and later that inning hit a Grand Slam off reliever Calvin Schiraldi in a Phillies 26-7 win over the Mets on June 11th, 1985.

In 2010, Phillies pitcher Roy Halladay became the 1st pitcher in the MLB modern era to pitch 250+ innings and have 30 or fewer walks,

On July 8th, 1952, the Phillies hosted their 1st MLB All Star game. The NL defeated the AL 3-2 in 5 innings. It's the 1st and only MLB All Star game in league history to end early due to rain.

Philly native Doug Allison played on the first fully-professional baseball team, the Cincinnati Red Stockings in 1868. Allison, as a catcher, was the 1st player to ever wear a glove.

Phillies pitcher Tommy Greene's 1991 no-hitter against the Montreal Expos was the 1st MLB no-hitter ever in Canada. Greene's no-hitter baseball cap sits in Cooperstown.

On July 8th, 2011, Phillies pitcher Juan Perez threw an immaculate inning (3 KOs on 9 pitches) in the 10th inning of a 3-2 win over the Atlanta

Braves. Perez was the 1st pitcher in MLB history to throw an immaculate inning in his 1st MLB win.

The Phillies played their 1st Major League game on May 1st, 1883, a 4-3 loss to the Providence Grays. They lost their first 8 games.

In 2010, Phillies catcher Carlos Ruiz became the 1st (and only) MLB catcher to catch two no-hitters in the same season.

Philly native Ernie Padgett turned the 1st-ever unassisted triple play in the National League on October 6th, 1923. The, Boston Braves infielder turned the triple play against his hometown Phillies. Padgett snared a Walter Holke line drive, touched second, and tagged the runner coming from first. It was just Padgett's 4th MLB game of his career.

Phillies pitcher Jim Konstanty was the National League MVP in 1950, the 1st relief pitcher to ever win the award.

The 1st-ever American League MVP was Lefty Grove of the Philadelphia A's in 1931.

Phillies 2B Manny Trillo was the 1st second baseman to win a Silver Slugger Award, winning in 1980.

Phillies 3B Mike Schmidt was the 1st third baseman to win a Silver Slugger Award, winning in 1980.

The Phillies played in the 1st-ever radio broadcasted MLB game on August 5th, 1921 in Pittsburgh, PA in an 8-5 loss to the Pirates.

The Phillies played in the 1st-ever night game in MLB history on May 24th, 1935 in a 2-1 loss in Cincinnati.

Phillies slugger Greg Luzinski was the team's 1st postseason designated hitter, opening the 1980 World Series vs Kansas City Royals as DH.

Connie Mack was the 1st Philadelphia sports figure inducted into his sport's Hall of Fame. Mack was inducted into the Baseball Hall of Fame in 1937 as Manager for the Philadelphia Athletics. The 1st sports figure inducted into the Hall of Fame as a player was Grover Cleveland "Pete" Alexander, inducted in 1938 as a Phillies Pitcher.

On June 23rd, 1971 Rick Wise became the 1st (and only) player in MLB history to hit two HRs in a game in which he threw a no-hitter.

Eagles Phirsts

Eagles QB Nick Foles was the 1st (and only) QB in NFL history to have a passer rating of 149+ in back to back games. In week 9 of 2013, Foles had a perfect 158.3 passer rating vs Oakland Raiders (his 7 TD game), and followed that up with a week 10 passer rating of 149.3 vs Green Bay Packers.

The back-to-back NFL Championships in 1948, and 1949 won by the Eagles were the only back-to-back titles ever won in the NFL by twin shutouts.

Eagles Hall of Famer Steve Van Buren was the 1st Philly sports star to have his number retired by one of the big 4 city sports teams. The Eagles retired his #15 in 1951.

Did you know... Eagles Hall of Famer Reggie White had his #92 retired by both the Eagles and the Green Bay Packers. He is the 1st NFL player to have his number retired by more than one team.

Bert Bell, an original owner of the Eagles, is the person who first introduced the concept of a college draft to fairly distribute incoming talent to the teams in the league.

In 1939, the Eagles played the Brooklyn Dodgers in the 1st-ever televised football game. The game, broadcasted by NBC, was played at Ebbetts Field in Brooklyn on October 22nd. The Dodgers won 23-14.

The Eagles participated in the 1st-ever televised championship game, defeating the Chicago Cardinals 7-0 on December 19th, 1948, in blizzard-like conditions.

During the 1998 football season, the Eagles became the 1st team in NFL history to be shutout twice at home in the same season by 30 points or more.

Eagles QB Nick Foles was the 1st NFL player ever to both throw and catch a TD pass in the same Super Bowl when he managed to do both in an Eagles 41-33 Super Bowl LII win.

Eagles legend Steve Van Buren was the first NFL player to rush for 1,000 yards in a season multiple times (1008 yards in 1947, 1146 yards in 1949).

Eagles Steve Van Buren was the 1st NFL player to rush for 10 TD's in a season, doing so three times before anyone else did it once.

In 1971, former Eagle Irv Cross became the 1st African-American full time network sports analyst when he was hired by CBS.

In 1994, Eagles running back Herschel Walker became the 1st player in NFL history to have a 90+yard rushing, receiving, and kick-return play in a single season.

On October 29th, 1933, Eagles Swede Hansen caught a 35 yard Roger Kirkman pass to score the Eagles 1st-ever TD in a 35-9 loss to the Green Bay Packers in Green Bay. It was the Eagles third game. They were shut out by a collective 81-0 in their first two games in existence.

In 1936, the Eagles made the 1st selection in the 1st-ever NFL Draft, selecting Jay Berwanger from the University of Chicago. Berwanger went to med school instead of signing.

Flyers Phirsts

The Flyers first NHL goal was scored by Bill Sutherland on October 11th, 1967 in a 5-1 road loss to the California Golden Seals.

On November 4th, 1967, Flyers Leon Rochefort notched the 1st hat trick in team history.

On November 20th, 1983, Flyers legend Bobby Clarke scored the 1st regular season overtime goal in team history, beating Pittsburgh Penguins goaltender Denis Herron 2:43 into overtime to give the Flyers a 5-4 win.

Flyers Orest Kindrachuk was the 1st Flyer to score on a penalty shot when he scored on November 9th, 1974 vs. Washington Capitals.

Flyers sniper Reggie Leach was the first aboriginal-born NHL player to ever have his name on the Stanley Cup. He was part of the Flyers 2nd Stanley Cup-winning team in 1975.

On February 10th, 2018 Flyers goalie Michal Neuvirth became the first goalie in NHL history to come into a game in relief during a shootout and win the game. Brian Elliott went down with an injury in the shootout's second round. Neuvirth stood tall against the Arizona Coyotes for 5 rounds and Nolan Patrick scored in the 7th round to seal the 4-3 win. Neuvy got the win giving up zero goals in zero minutes played.

On September 1st, 1968 goaltender Bobby Taylor became the 1st Free Agent signed by the Flyers.

Flyers goaltender Ron Hextall became the 1st goalie in NHL history to shoot the puck into the opponent's net when he scored an open net goal against the Boston Bruins on December 8th, 1987.

Flyers goalie Ron Hextall became the 1st goalie in NHL history to shoot the puck into the opposition net during the postseason when he scored an open net goal against the Washington Capitals on April 11th, 1989 in an 8-5 playoff win. The goal also made Hextall the 1st (and only) NHL goalie to shoot the puck into an opposition net multiple times.

The Flyers 1st expansion draft pick was goaltender Bernie Parent. Their 1st Entry Draft pick was Serge Bernier.

Flyers goalie Pelle Lindbergh was the 1st NHL goalie to bring a water bottle onto the ice during the game, doing so to address dehydration issues.

Flyers goalie Pelle Lindbergh was the 1st European goaltender to win the NHL's Vezina Trophy.

Flyers goalie Pelle Lindbergh was posthumously selected for the NHL's 1986 All Star game, the first posthumous All Star selection in a North American major league.

Sixers Phirsts

The Sixers boasted the Sixth Man Award, Coach of the Year, Defensive Player of the Year, and NBA MVP in 2001. They are the only NBA team to ever garner these 4 awards in the same season.

Sixers Darryl Dawkins was the 1st NBA player selected directly from high school.

Philadelphia Warriors' Wilt Chamberlain was the 1st (and only) NBA player to hit the century mark in an NBA game when he scored 100 points in a 169-147 win over the New York Knicks on March 2nd, 1962 in Hershey, PA, in front of a meager 4,124 spectators and no broadcast tape.

Franklin Field was the 1st two-tiered stadium in the country and also sported the 1st scoreboard.

What's in a name...

The best nicknames from Philly's favorite sports teams.

Phillies...

Ryan Howard – Big Piece

Chase Utley – the Man

Jimmy Rollins – J-roll

Carlos Ruiz – Chooch

Cole Hamels – Hollywood

Roy Halladay – Doc

Brad Lidge – Lights Out

Shane Victorino – Flyin' Hawaiian

Pat Burrell – Pat the bat

Mitch Williams – Wild Thing

Darren Daulton – Dutch

Len Dykstra – Nails, Dude

Vance Worley – Vanimal

Tom Gordon – Flash

Von Hayes – 5 for 1

Gary Matthews – Sarge

Larry Bowa – Gnat

Tug McGraw – Tugger

Steve Carlton – Lefty

Pete Rose – Charlie Hustle

Steve Bedrosian – Bedrock

Octavio Rojas – Cookie

Garry Maddox – Secretary of defense

Greg Luzinski – Bull

Bake McBride - Shake and Bake

Dick Allen - Crash

Richie Ashburn - Whitey

Willie Jones – Puddin' head

Eagles...

Gang Green

The Birds

Pete Retzlaff – Pistol Pete, the Baron

Norm Van Brocklin – The Dutchman

Chuck Bednarik – Concrete Charley, 60 minute man

Brian Dawkins – Weapon X, Wolverine

Nick Foles – Nicky Six

Randall Cunningham – the Ultimate Weapon

Terrell Owens – T.O.

Bill Hewitt – Stinky

Ron Jaworski – Jaws, Polish Rifle

Earl Neale – Greasy

Jeremiah Trotter – Axe Man

Steve Van Buren – Wham Bam

Reggie White – Minister of defense

Ricky Watters – Running Watters

Andre Waters – Dirty Waters

Jalen Mills – Green Goblin

Jevon Kearse – Freak

LeSean McCoy – Shady

Freddie Mitchell – FredEx

Marion Campbell – Swamp Fox

Izel Jenkins – Toast

Flyers...

Dave Schultz – Hammer, Zeus

Bob Kelly – the Hound

Don Saleski – Big Bird

Rick MacLeish – Hawk

Bill Barber – Arnie

Broad Street Bullies

Orange and Black

Fly Guys

Legion of Doom

Crazy 8's line

LCB line

Rod Brind Amour – Rod the bod

Ilya Bryzgalov – Mr. Universe

Dan Carcillo – Car Bomb

Antero Niitymaki – Frank (niity)

Robert Esche – Chico

Eric Desjardins – Rico

Andre Dupont – Moose

Brian Elliott – Moose

Todd Fedoruk – Fridge

Valtteri Filppula – Flipper

Bill Flett – Cowboy

Ron Flockhart – Flockey hockey

Peter Forsberg – Foppa, Peter the great

Shayne Gostisbehere – Ghost

Larry Goodenough – Izzy

Michal Handzus – Zeus

Ron Hextall – Hexy

Jaromir Jagr – Jags

Reggie Leach – Riverton Rifle

John LeClair – Johnny Vermont

Ken Linseman – the Rat

Mark Recchi – Rex, Wrecking Ball

Jeremy Roenick – J.R.

Fred Shero – Fog

Wayne Simmonds – Simmer, Wayne Train

Max Talbot – Mad Max

Chris Therien – Bundy

John Vanbiesbrouck – Beezer

James Van Riemsdyk – JVR

Jake Voracek – Scoracek

Craig Berube – Chief

Bobby Taylor – Chief

Bob Dailey – the Count

Sixers...

Julius Erving – Dr. J

Allen Iverson – the Answer, A.I.

Joe Bryant – Jellybean

Lloyd Free – World B Free

Joel Embiid – the Process

Charles Barkley – Round Mound of Rebound, Sir Charles

Darryl Dawkins – Chocolate Thunder

Wilt Chamberlain – Wilt the stilt, Big Dipper

Nik Stauskas – Sauce Castillo

Fred Carter – Mad Dog

Billy Cunningham – Kangaroo Kid

Andrew Toney – Boston Strangler

Brotherly Love

in the City of Brotherly Love...

Orator and Taylor Shaffer – Athletics 1890

Ed and Tom Delahanty – Phillies 1894

Bill and Roy Thomas – Phillies 1902

Dino and Lou Chiozza – Phillies 1935

Garvin and Granny Hamner – Phillies 1945

Steve and Ebert Van Buren – Eagles 1951

Alex and Walt Kellner – Athletics 1952-53

Billy and Bobby Shantz – Athletics 1954-55

Dave and Dennis Bennett – Phillies 1964

Wayne and Larry Hillman – Flyers 1969-71

Joe and Jim Watson – Flyers 1973-78

Ron and Rich Sutter – Flyers 1983-86

Ty and Koy Detmer - Eagles 1997

Kimmo and Jussi Timonen - Flyers 2007 (*roster only)

Shawn and Stacy Andrews – Eagles 2009 (*roster only)

Jrue and Justin Holliday – Sixers 2013

Brayden and Luke Schenn – Flyers 2013-16

50 from Philly

Editor's note: There are some truly great athletes that are synonymous with Philly that aren't included here (Orel Hershiser, Joe Frazier, Carl Lewis etc) as they were born elsewhere. This list contains some of the best that were BORN in the metro Philly area.

Herb Adderley (b. Philly – football) Only player to appear in four of the first six Super Bowls, five-time Pro Bowler, three-time Super Bowl Champ, Green Bay Packers Hall of Fame, Pro Football Hall of Fame.

Doug Allison (b. Philly – baseball) played on the first fully-professional baseball team, the Cincinnati Red Stockings (1868). Allison, as a catcher, was the 1st player to ever wear a glove.

Ruben Amaro, jr. (b. Philly – baseball) Phillies batboy, OF, AGM, and GM.

Paul Arizin (b. Philly – basketball) Arizin played his entire NBA career with his hometown Philadelphia Warriors. The Villanova star was a ten-time NBA All Star, two-time scoring champ, 1952 NBA All Star Game MVP, and named to the NBA's 50th Anniversary Team. Arizin is in both the College Hall of Fame and the Naismith Memorial Basketball Hall of Fame.

Bert Bell (b. Philly – football) NFL Commissioner 1945-59, Eagles Head Coach 1936-40, Eagles Hall of Fame, Pro Football Hall of Fame, created the NFL Draft, founded the Maxwell Club. Bert Bell Award given to NFL Player of the Year by the Maxwell Club.

Mohini Bhardwaj (b. Philly – Olympic gymnast) Mohini Bhardwaj won a Silver Medal with the US Women's Gymnastics Team at the 2004 Summer

Olympics in Athens, Greece. She is the first Indian-American gymnast to medal at the Olympics.

Tyrell Biggs (b. Philly – boxer) Tyrell Biggs was a Super Heavyweight Gold Medal-winning boxer at the 1984 Summer Olympic Games in Los Angeles. He also won Gold as a Super Heavyweight at the 1982 Munich World Championships. He had 20 KOs in 40 professional fights.

Kobe Bryant (b. Philly – basketball) Kobe Bryant was simply one of the greatest basketball players to ever play the game. He is the 1st guard in NBA history to play 20 seasons. The 18-time NBA All Star also holds the NBA record for Most Seasons playing for one franchise for the entire career. Bryant won 5 NBA Championships.

Joe Bryant (b. Philly – basketball) Joe Bryant was more than just Kobe's father. Jellybean played 4 seasons for the Sixers after his standout career with LaSalle.

Roy Campanella (b. Philly – baseball) One of the greatest catchers of all time. Eight-time All Star, three-time NL MVP. His career was cut short by a tragic car accident that left him paralyzed.

Fred Carter (b. Philly – basketball) "Mad Dog" Carter played parts of six seasons with the Sixers averaging 35.4 minutes/game, and 18.8 points.

Wilt Chamberlain (b. Philly – basketball) Wilt Chamberlain was the most dominating basketball player ever. Wilt played for both the Philadelphia Warriors and the Philadelphia 76ers. The Warriors, Sixers and Lakers all retired his #13. Chamberlain is in both the College Hall of Fame and the Naismith Memorial Basketball Hall of Fame.

Jeff Chandler (b. Philly – boxer) 5'7" Joltin' Jeff had a professional record of 33 wins 2 losses and 2 draws with 18 wins by KOs. Held the bantamweight title and was inducted into the International Boxing HOF.

Angelo Dundee (b. Philly – boxing trainer) Angelo Dundee was one of the greatest boxing trainers and cornermen of all-time. His stable of boxers include Muhammad Ali, Sugar Ray Leonard, George Foreman, and Trevor Berbick. Dundee trained Russell Crowe for his role in Cinderella Man. Dundee was inducted into the International Boxing Hall of Fame in 1994.

Tyreke Evans (b. Chester, PA – basketball) Tyreke Evans was a fourth overall selection of the Sacramento Kings in the 2009 NBA Draft. He was the 2010 NBA Rookie of the Year, NBA Rookie Challenge co-MVP in 2010 and is still currently playing in the NBA.

Irving Fryar (b. Mt. Holly, NJ – football) five-time Pro Bowler, 1st player to record a TD in 17 straight seasons.

Johnny Gaudreau (b. Salem, NJ) "Johnny Hockey" 2014 Hobey Baker Award Winner, three-time All Star, Calder Trophy Finalist, Lady Byng Memorial Trophy winner 2017.

Eddie George (b. Philly – football) 1995 Heisman Award Winner, four-time Pro Bowler, NFL Offensive Rookie of the Year '96, 10,441 career rush yds.

Tom Gola (b. Philly – basketball) Tom Gola was considered one of the all-time greatest in NCAA history. He was a five-time NBA All Star and won an NBA Championship with the Philadelphia Warriors. Gola is in both the College Hall of Fame and the Naismith Memorial Basketball Hall of Fame.

Matt Goukas – (b. Philly – basketball) Goukas was drafted 9th overall in the 1966 NBA Draft by the Sixers. Goukas won 2 NBA championships with Sixers, as a player in 1967, and assistant coach in 1983.

Randy Grossman (b. Philly – football) four-time Super Bowl Winner with the Pittsburgh Steelers.

Mark Gubicza – (b. Philly – baseball) Two-time All Star, 1985 World Series Champ. Inducted into Kansas City Royals Hall of Fame.

Richard Hamilton (b. Coatesville, PA – basketball) Rip Hamilton was the 7th overall selection in the 1999 NBA Draft by the Washington Wizards. He won an NBA Title with the Detroit Pistons in 2004, and was a three-time NBA All Star. Hamilton was noted for the clear plastic protective face mask he wore. His #32 was retired by the Detroit Pistons.

Brendan Hansen (b. Haverford – swimmer) Brendan Hansen is a 6-time Olympic medalist winning 3 Gold, 1 Silver, and 2 Bronze. He has won 25 medals in major international competitions.

Franco Harris (b. Fort Dix, NJ – football) NFL Offensive Rookie of the Year 1972, nine-time Pro Bowler, Super Bowl IX MVP, four-time Super Bowl Champ, Pro Football Hall of Fame.

Marvin Harrison (b. Philly – football) One of the greatest wide receivers ever. Eight-time Pro Bowler, Super Bowl XLI Champ, Indianapolis Colts Ring of Honor, Pro Football Hall of Fame 2016.

Bernard Hopkins (b. Philly – boxer) "The Executioner" was one of the greatest boxers of the last quarter-century. He is the oldest boxer in history (49) to win a world championship.

Reggie Jackson (b. Wyncote, Pa – baseball) Mr. October, fourteen-time All Star, 1973 AL MVP, 1973, 1977 World Series MVP, four-time AL HR leader, five-time World Series Winner, #9 retired by Oakland A's, #44 retired by New York Yankees, inducted into Hall of Fame in 1993.

John B. Kelly, sr. (b. Philly – Olympic rower) Jack Kelly was a three-time Olympic rowing Gold Medalist. Kelly was the father of Grace Kelly, (movie star and Princess of Monaco) and Olympic rower John B. Kelly jr.

Leroy Kelly (b. Philly – football) Two-time rushing leader, six-time Pro Bowler, Pro Football Hall of Fame, Bert Bell Award 1968.

Tommy Loughran (b. Philly – boxer) Loughran was a World Light Heavyweight Champ. He was top ten all-time in his weight class. He had 121 wins, 32 losses, and 14 draws and 14 KOs.

Kyle Lowry (b. Philly – basketball) Kyle Lowry was a graduate of Cardinal Dougherty HS and played under Jay Wright at Villanova. Lowery is still an active player in the NBA and has been an All Star each of the last four seasons (2015-2018)

Aaron McKie (B. Philly – basketball) Aaron McKie was a Temple University standout. He won the NBA's 6th Man Award in 2001 while with the Sixers. McKie spent six seasons as Sixers assistant coach.

Earl Monroe (b. Philly – basketball) Earl the Pearl was the 2nd overall pick in the 1967 NBA Draft. His number was retired by both the Baltimore Bullets, and the New York Knicks. Monroe was NBA Rookie of the Year in 1968, and a four-time All Star.

Jamie Moyer (b. Sellersville, PA – baseball) Jamie Moyer's career spanned four decades (1986-2012). He pitched for eight teams in his 25 year career. He is the oldest Major Leaguer to record a win and an RBI.

Matthew Saad Muhammad (b. Philly – boxer) born Maxwell Antonio Loach, Matthew Saad Muhammad overcame incredible childhood traumas to become a WBC Light heavyweight champ. He had 32 KOs in 68 professional fights.

Jameer Nelson (b. Chester, PA – basketball) Jameer Nelson was the National College Player of the Year with the St. Joe's Hawks in 2004. Nelson was an NBA All Star in 2009.

Vince Papale (b. Glenolden, Pa - football) the oldest NFL rookie (30yrs old) to never play college ball. Eagles walk-on, played for Philadelphia Bell. Feature film "Invincible" with Mark Walhberg based on Papale's exploits in the NFL.

Mike Piazza (b. Norristown, Pa – baseball) twelve-time All Star, ten-time Silver Slugger, NL Rookie of the Year 1993, New York Mets Hall of Fame, #31 retired by NYM, Baseball Hall of Fame 2016.

Mike Powell (b. Philly – Olympic Track and Field) Mike Powell won two Gold Medals at the World Championships in Long Jump, and a Silver Medal at both the 1988 Summer Olympic Games in Seoul, and the 1992 Summer Olympic Games in Barcelona.

Jack Ramsey (b. coach – basketball) Jack Ramsey is among the top ten NBA coaches of all time. He coached the Sixers for four seasons, won an NBA title with the Portland Trail Blazers, and was NBA All Star Head Coach in 1978. Ramsey is in both the Naismith Memorial Basketball Hall of Fame, and the College Basketball Hall of Fame.

Merril Reese (b. Philly – football broadcaster) Voice of the Eagles since 1977, longest tenured play-by-play announcer in NFL.

Mike Richter (b. Abington, PA – hockey) Grew up in Flourtown, PA. Three-time All Star, 1994 Stanley Cup winner, 1994 NHL All Star Game MVP, US Hockey Hall of Fame 2008, Silver Medal 2002 Olympics, his #35 retired by New York Rangers in 2004.

Mike Rozier (b. Camden, NJ – football) 1983 Heisman Award Winner, 1983 Maxwell Award, two-time Pro Bowler.

Matt Ryan (b. Exton, Pa – football) "Matty Ice", four-time Pro Bowler, NFL Offensive Player of the Year 2016, NFL MVP 2016, Bert Bell Award 2016.

Dawn Staley (b. Philly – women's basketball) Staley was a three-time Olympic Gold Medalist with the US Women's Basketball Team. She was the United States flag-bearer at the 2004 Summer Olympic Games Opening Ceremony, in Athens, Greece. Staley was inducted into the Naismith Memorial Basketball Hall of Fame in 2013.

Mike Trout (b. Vineland, NJ – baseball) The "Millville Meteor", six-time All Star, two-time AL MVP, five-time Silver Slugger, AL Rookie of the Year, AL RBI Leader 2014.

Jersey Joe Walcott (b. Pennsauken, NJ – boxer) Arnold Raymond Cream, AKA Jersey Joe Walcott, was a heavyweight boxer who, upon winning the World Heavyweight Title at age 37, was the oldest heavyweight boxer to do so (since surpassed by George Foreman). Walcott had 32 KOs in 71 fights.

Rasheed Wallace (b. Philly – basketball) 4th overall pick in the 1995 NBA Draft. 1993 USA Today's High School Player of the Year. "Sheed" was a four-time NBA All Star.

Erik Williams (b. Philly – football) four-time Pro Bowler, three-time Super Bowl Champ.

And the Award goes to...

Major League Baseball

MOST VALUABLE PLAYER

Chuck Klein 1932

Jim Konstanty 1950

Mike Schmidt 1980, 81, 86

Ryan Howard 2006

Jimmy Rollins 2007

CY YOUNG AWARD

Steve Carlton 1972, 77, 80, 82

John Denny 1983

Steve Bedrosian 1987

Roy Halladay 2010

MANAGER OF THE YEAR

Larry Bowa 2001

ROOKIE OF THE YEAR

Jack Sanford 1957   Scott Rolen 1997

Dick Allen 1964   Ryan Howard 2005

ROBERTO CLEMENTE AWARD

Greg Luzinski 1978

Garry Maddox 1986

Jimmy Rollins 2014

SILVER SLUGGER AWARD

Mike Schmidt 1980, 1981, 1982, 1983, 1984, 1986

Manny Trillo 1980, 1981

Juan Samuel 1987

Darren Daulton 1992

Lenny Dykstra 1993

Bobby Abreau 2004

Ryan Howard 2006

Chase Utley 2006, 2007, 2008, 2009

Jimmy Rollins 2007

GOLD GLOVE AWARD

Bobby Wine 1963

Ruben Amaro 1964

Bill White 1966

Larry Bowa 1972, 78

Garry Maddox 1975, 76, 77, 78, 79, 80, 81, 82

Jim Kaat 1976, 77

Mike Schmidt 1976, 77, 78, 79, 80, 81, 82, 83, 84, 86

Bob Boone 1978, 79

Many Trillo 1979, 81, 82

Steve Carlton 1981

Scott Rolen 1998, 00, 01

Mike Lieberthal 1999

Bobby Abreau 2005

Jimmy Rollins 2007, 08, 09, 12

Aaron Rowand 2007

Shane Victorino 2008, 09, 10

Placido Polanco 2011

HANK AARON AWARD

Ryan Howard 2006

COMEBACK PLAYER OF THE YEAR

Brad Lidge 2008

WORLD SERIES MVP

Mike Schmidt 1980

Cole Hamels 2008

NLCS MVP

Manny Trillo 1980

Gary Matthews 1983

Curt Schilling 1993

Cole Hamels 2008

Ryan Howard 2009

ALL STAR GAME MVP

Johnny Callison 1964

RELIEF MAN AWARD

Al Holland 1983   Brad Lidge 2008

Steve Bedrosian 1987

National Football League

SUPER BOWL MVP

Nick Foles 2018

PRO BOWL MVP

Chuck Bednarik 1954

Reggie White 1987

Randall Cunningham 1989

Nick Foles 2014

AP MVP

Norm Van Brocklin 1960

Pro Football Writers Assoc NFL MVP Award

Randall Cunningham 1990

AP NFL COACH OF THE YEAR

Buck Shaw 1960

Ray Rhodes 1995

Andy Reid 2002

AP DEFENSIVE PLAYER OF THE YEAR

Reggie White 1987

AP COMEBACK PLAYER OF THE YEAR

Michael Vick 2010

WALTER PAYTON NFL MAN OF THE YEAR AWARD

Harold Carmichael 1980   Chris Long 2018

Troy Vincent 2002

FEDEX AIR PLAYER OF THE YEAR

Carson Wentz 2017

FEDEX GROUND PLAYER OF THE YEAR

LeSean McCoy 2011

National Hockey League

FOSTER HEWITT MEMORIAL

Mike Emrick 2008

Gene Hart 1997

LESTER PATRICK TROPHY

Bob Clarke 1980

Fred Shero   1980

Ed Snider   1980

Keith Allen 1988

Bud Poile 1989

Mike Emrick 2004

Paul Holmgren 2014

Mark Howe 2016

BILL MASTERTON TROPHY

Bobby Clarke 1972

Tim Kerr 1989

Ian Laperriere 2011

CONN SMYTHE TROPHY

Bernie Parent 1974, 1975

Reg Leach 1976

Ron Hextall 1987

FRANK J SELKE TROPHY

Bobby Clarke 1983

Dave Poulin 1987

HART MEMORIAL TROPHY

Bobby Clarke 1973, 75, 76

Eric Lindros 1995

JACK ADAMS

Fred Shero 1974

Pat Quinn 1980

Mike Keenan 1985

Bill Barber 2001

TED LINDSAY AWARD (formerly Lester B. Pearson award)

Bobby Clarke 1974

Eric Lindros 1995

VEZINA TROPHY

Bernie Parent 1974 (tied w/ Tony Esposito), 1975

Pelle Lindbergh 1985

Ron Hextall 1987

WILLIAM M. JENNINGS TROPHY

Bob Froese/Darren Jensen 1986

Roman Cechmanek/Robert Esche 2003 (tied w/M. Brodeur)

NHL PLUS/MINUS AWARD

Mark Howe 1986

John LeClair 1997, 99

National Basketball Association

MOST VALUABLE PLAYER

Wilt Chamberlain 1966-68   Moses Malone 1983

Julius Erving 1981   Allen Iverson 2001

FINALS MVP

Moses Malone 1983

DEFENSIVE PLAYER OF THE YEAR

Dikembe Mutombo 2001

ROOKIE OF THE YEAR

Allen Iverson 1997

Michael Carter Williams 2014

Ben Simmons 2018

NBA 6th MAN

Bobby Jones 1983

Aaron McKie 2001

MOST IMPROVED PLAYER OF THE YEAR

Dana Barros 1995

COACH OF THE YEAR

Dolph Schayes 1966

Larry Brown 2001

NBA SPORTSMANSHIP

Eric Snow 2000

J WALTER KENNEDY CITIZENSHIP AWARD

Julius Erving 1983

Dikembe Mutombo 2001

Samuel Dalembert 2010

NBA SCORING CHAMPION

Wilt Chamberlain 1965, 66

Allen Iverson 1999, 01, 02, 05

Philly's Greatest Voices...

Phillies

Richie Ashburn (1963-97) Richie Ashburn is one of the most beloved sports voices in Philly history. Ashburn spent 34 seasons in the Phillies booth after his Hall of Fame baseball career. Ashburn was also a regular contributor to The Philadelphia Bulletin and The Philadelphia Daily News newspapers. Whitey Ashburn passed away on Sept 9th, 1997 following a Phillies-Mets game at Shea Stadium. The Phillies honored Whitey by naming their entertainment area at Citizen's Bank Park "Ashburn Alley."

Bill Campbell (1963-70) Bill Campbell was a Philly sports icon, his unique voice covering an array of broadcasts. Along with his time in the Phillies booth, Campbell did Eagles play-by-play from 1952-66, and the Sixers from 1972-81. Campbell was the voice of the Philadelphia Warriors NBA team from their inception in 1946 until their departure for San Francisco in 1962. Campbell was part of the radio broadcast for Wilt Chamberlain's record-breaking 100 point game in Hershey, PA. Campbell was also an original WIP sports talk radio personality when the station turned to an all sports format in 1987.

Harry Kalas (1971-2009) It's Outta Here! Harry Kalas replaced the extremely popular Bill Campbell for the Phillies play-by-play in 1971. His MLB debut with the Phillies was the debut of Veteran's Stadium.

Kalas had just begun his 38th season with the Phillies broadcast team in 2009, after the Phillies had won their 2nd World Series the previous fall. On April 8th, 2009 as part of the pre-game ceremony where the team received their World Series Championship rings, Kalas was honored by throwing out the game's first pitch. It was Kalas's last home game with the Phillies. On April 13th, 2009, the day before the Phillies were scheduled to go to the White House following their World Series win, Kalas collapsed in the broadcast booth prior to the game vs the Nationals and died a short time later. Kalas was also known for his work with NFL Films, replacing the legendary John Facenda.

Andy Musser (1976-2001) Andy Musser teamed with Richie Ashburn and Harry Kalas doing Phillies TV and radio play-by-play for 21 consecutive seasons. Musser continued on with the Phillies for 4 more seasons after Richie Ashburn's passing. Over his career, Musser also did radio play-by-play for the Eagles, Sixers, and Villanova basketball.

By Saam (1939-49, 1955-75) Byron Saam was the first full-time broadcaster for the Philadelphia Athletics in 1938, and took on the same job with the Phillies in 1939. Both the Phils and the A's played out of Shibe Park. Since away games weren't broadcasted, Saam was able to do play-by-play for both teams, a dual role he held for a dozen years. During his tenure, neither team made the playoffs. Its estimated By Saam broadcasted over 4,000 losses collectively, more than any other baseball announcer. By Saam also did radio broadcasts for the Philadelphia Warriors in the NBA. Saam, along with Bill Campbell, broadcasted Wilt Chamberlain's record 100-point game in Hershey, PA . On November 26th, 1953, Saam broadcasted the 1st nationally-televised NFL Thanksgiving Day Game, which featured the Detroit Lions and the Green Bay Packers.

Chris Wheeler (1977-2013) Chris Wheeler was the Phillies assistant director of publicity and public relations for six years before joining the broadcast booth for the 1977 season. Wheeler remained a fixture in the booth for the next 37 years. Wheeler also ran the Phillies Dream Week from 1983-99.

Did you know...

... Harry Kalas broadcasted the 1st-ever indoor MLB baseball game when he called the Houston Astros home opener and Houston Astrodome debut on April 12th, 1965. Kalas also broadcasted the 1st and last games at Veteran's Stadium, and the Citizen's Bank Park debut.

... Harry Kalas narrated the self-guided tour audio for both the US Mint and the Gateway Arch in St. Louis.

... Chris Wheeler was once an airborne traffic reporter.

Eagles

Merrill Reese (1977-present) Merrill Reese has been the voice of the Eagles for over 40 years. He is the longest-tenured play-by-play announcer in the NFL. Reese's first full time season doing play-by-play was the NFL's first 16-game season. Reese has worked with 5 color commentators (Herb Adderly, Jim Barniak, Bill Bergey, Stan Walters, and Mike Quick). He has seen 10 different head coaches, 8 Hall of Famers, 39 QBs, 3 team owners, and 650 regular season games.

Did you know...

... Merrill Reese has never missed a single Eagles game since his 1977 debut!

Flyers

Gene Hart (1967-95) Gene Hart was the iconic voice of the Flyers from the team's inception during the 1967-68 season through the end of the 1994-95 season. Hart called over 2,000 NHL games, 6 Stanley Cup Finals including the 1974 and 1975 Cup winners, and 5 NHL All Star games. Gene Hart taught the game of hockey to a sports-crazed town, and the incredible turnout for the Flyers Stanley Cup parade in the spring of 1974 was undoubtedly due in part to the passion Hart had for the Flyers, and how legions of fans fed off that passion. Gene Hart was inducted into the

Hockey Hall of Fame in 1997. Not too bad for a Jersey high school history teacher. Good night, good hockey!

Mike Emrick (1988-93) Doc Emrick did Flyers play-by-play for 5 seasons, paired with Bill Clement for four of those seasons. Emrick has become a national hockey broadcasting icon since his early days with the Flyers. Emrick has done Olympic Games, NFL games, NCAA basketball games, and National Lacrosse League games. He's worked with NBC, CBS, ABC, TNT, ESPN, FOX, Versus, OLN, SportsChannel, and Prism. Emrick, along with colleagues Eddie Olczyk and Ray Ferraro have provided play-by-play commentary on all EA Sports hockey games since NHL 15.

Jim Jackson (1993-present) Jim Jackson has been broadcasting Flyers games since he began doing Flyers radio games in 1993. Two seasons later he began doing TV broadcasts and is still going strong. Jackson has carved a niche for himself as another icon of Philly sports. In 2007, Jackson added pre and post-game Phillies radio broadcasts to his repertoire. J.J. now does midgame play-by-play for Phillies home games. Jackson had huge shoes to fill taking over for legendary Gene Hart. Jackson has earned a spot among the best voices in Philly sports history.

Did you know...

... Gene Hart's daughter, the lovely Lauren Hart, not only sings the National Anthem or God Bless America before every Flyers home game, but as a tribute to her Dad, wears a #68 Flyers sweater, Gene Hart's age at his passing.

... Mike Emrick has a Ph.D. in communications from Bowling Green University, hence the nickname "Doc".

... Mike Emrick is a founding member and current President of the NHL Pronunciation Guide, a guide utilized by NHL broadcasters to pronounce difficult names of NHL players.

Sixers

Marc Zumoff (1983-present) Mark Zumoff has been the Sixers play-by-play guy for a quarter century. Prior to that he did pre/post game and halftime broadcast duties. Besides his stellar broadcast career with the Sixers, Zumoff worked for NBC during the Rio Olympics and has done Big 5 basketball, soccer, Lacrosse, and Villanova football and basketball. Zumoff has 18 Mid-Atlantic Emmys on his mantel.

Give us some color...

The Best of Philly's Color Commentators

Chris Wheeler (Phillies 1977-13)

Kent Tekulve (Phillies 1992-97)

Larry Andersen (Phillies 1998-present)

Gary Matthews (Phillies 2007-13)

Bill Bergey (Eagles 1982-83)

Stan Walters (Eagles 1984-97)

Mike Quick (Eagles 1998-present)

Bobby Taylor (Flyers 1976-92)

Bill Clement (Flyers 1989-92, 2007-present)

Gary Dornhoefer (Flyers 1992-06)

Steve Coates (Flyers 1992-present)

Keith Jones (Flyers 2006-present)

Chris Therien (Flyers 2014-18)

Steve Mix (Sixers 1994-07)

Alaa Abdelnaby (Sixers 2015-present)

Put Me In, Coach!

Phillies

Eddie Sawyer (1948-52, 1958-60) In 1950, Sawyer led the Phillies to their first pennant in 35 years. Sawyer quit as Phillies Manager just one game into the 1960 season.

Danny Ozark (1973-79) Danny Ozark led the Phillies to three consecutive division titles from 1976-78.

Dallas Green (1979-81) Dallas Green took over for Danny Ozark during the 1979 season and led the Phillies to their first-ever World Series Championship in 1980.

John Vukovich (coach 1988-04, manager 1987) Vuk was beloved in Philly for his blue-collar work ethic both as a player and a coach. He is one of only three Phillies to appear in the World Series with the team as both a player and a coach.

Jim Fregosi (1991-96) Fregosi led a Macho Row group of ballplayers to within two wins of a World Championship in 1993. The team led their division for 161 out of 162 games.

Larry Bowa (coach 1989-96, manager 2001-04) Fiery Larry Bowa was on the Phillies coaching staff during their Cinderella run to the World Series in 1993. Bowa took over the reins as Skipper in 2001 and was named Coach of the Year.

Charlie Manuel (2005-13) Charlie Manuel was the Skipper for the greatest era in Phillies history. Manuel led the Phils to their second World Championship in 2008 and a follow-up trip to the World Series in 2009.

Eagles

Earl "Greasy" Neale (1941-50) NFL Hall of Famer Greasy Neale coached the Eagles to back-to-back NFL championships in 1948 and 1949, the only back-to-back NFL championships by twin shutouts. Neale, a two-sport star also played MLB with the Phillies.

Buck Shaw (1958-60) Shaw took over a last-place Eagles team and in three seasons led them to their 3rd NFL championship in 1960, defeating the Green Bay Packers 17-13. It was the only playoff loss ever suffered by legendary Packers coach Vince Lombardi.

Dick Vermeil (1976-82) Dick Vermeil led the Eagles to their first Super Bowl appearance in 1980 but fell to the Oakland Raiders 27-10. In his 3rd year in Philly, Vermeil led the team to the postseason for the 1st time since their 1960 NFL championship.

Buddy Ryan (1986-90) Buddy Ryan was a great defensive mind and is credited with developing the 46 defense. He coached the Vikings vaunted "Purple People Eaters", the Chicago Bears "Monsters of the Midway" and put together the Eagles "Gang Green" defense. As a head coach, he was 0-3 in the postseason with the Birds.

Jim Johnson (def coord. 1999-08) Legendary Jim Johnson was one of the NFL's greatest defensive coordinators. His defense amassed 342 sacks from 2000-07, and in 2001, became just the 4th NFL team to go an entire 16-game season without allowing more than 21 points in a game. Their 34-game streak of 21 points or under is 2nd best in NFL history.

Andy Reid (1999-12) Andy Reid led the Eagles to five NFC Championship games and a Super Bowl XXXIX appearance. Reid has the dubious distinction of being the NFL's all-time wins leader to not have an NFL championship.

Doug Pederson (2016-present) Doug Pederson went from being called the least qualified head coach in the NFL to a Super Bowl Champion head coach in just two seasons. Pederson is one of only four NFLers to win a Super Bowl as both a player and head coach (Tom Flores, Tony Dungy, Mike Ditka). Both of Pederson's Super Bowl rings have come at the expense of the New England Patriots.

Flyers

Fred Shero (1971-78) Hall of Fame coach Fred "the fog" Shero led the Flyers to 3 consecutive Stanley Cup Finals, winning the Cup in 1974 and 1975. Shero was an NHL innovator studying film of opponents, having players utilize in-season strength-training, employing "systems", and hiring the NHL's 1st full-time assistant coach (Mike Nykoluk 1972).

Pat Quinn (1977-82) Pat Quinn was hired as an assistant coach for the Flyers by Fred Shero. Quinn became the Flyers' head coach midway through the 1878-79 season. During his 1st full season as Flyers head coach, the team went on a record-breaking 35 game unbeaten streak (25-0-10) that still stands today. He led the Flyers to their 4th Stanley Cup Finals series, falling to the NY Islanders in 6 games. Quinn won the Jack Adams Award that season as NHL Coach of the Year.

Mike Keenan (1984-88) "Iron Mike" Keenan made his NHL coaching debut in 1984 when the Flyers hired him away from the University of Toronto. He led the Flyers to the team's 5th Stanley Cup Finals appearance where they fell to a star-studded Edmonton Oilers team. Kennan took the team to its 6th Stanley Cup Finals in 1987 losing to the same Edmonton Oilers in a gripping 7-game series.

Bill Barber (2000-02) Hall of Famer Bill Barber only coached the Flyers for a season and a half but he won the Jack Adams Award as NHL Coach of the Year in his only full season as head coach. Barber coached the

Flyers AHL affiliate Philadelphia Phantoms to their 1st AHL championship.

Peter Laviolette (2009-14) Peter Laviolette led the Flyers to their 8th Stanley Cup Finals appearance in 2010. The Flyers were defeated by the Chicago Black Hawks. The Flyers were down 3 games to none vs the Boston Bruins in the 2010 conference semi-finals, and were trailing game four 3-0. Laviolette called a time out and told his team to take it one goal at a time. They battled back to win the game and went on to take the series in seven games.

Sixers

Dolph Schayes (1963-67) NBA Hall of Famer Dolph Schayes was a player for the Syracuse Nationals/Philadelphia 76ers and became player/coach the year the team moved to Philly. Schayes was named Coach of the Year in 1966 when the Sixers finished 1st in the Eastern Division with a 55-25 record.

Alex Hannum (1966-68) Alex Hannum took over the Sixers when Dolph Schayes took a job with the NBA. Hannum took a 55-win 1st place team to a 68-13 record and an NBA Championship title. The Sixers 1966-67 team is widely regarded to be one of the greatest NBA teams ever assembled.

Jack Ramsey (1968-72) Hall of Famer Jack Ramsey coached the Sixers for 4 seasons, making the postseason in three of them. The season prior to Ramsey taking over as coach, Ramsey was the team's General Manager for the 1967 Championship team. Ramsey was forced to trade Wilt Chamberlain and Chet Walker during his tenure as coach/GM, and the Sixers started a steady decline that would bottom out in 1972 with their 9-73 team the year after Ramsey left.

Billy Cunningham (1977-85) Hall of Famer Billy C coached the Sixers for 8 consecutive winning seasons finishing with a .698 winning pct., 3 NBA Finals appearances and an NBA Championship in 1983. Cunningham reached 300 wins and 400 wins faster than any other coach in NBA history. The Kangaroo Kid won an NBA Championship with the Sixers as both a player (1967) and a coach (1983).

Larry Brown (1997-03) Hall of Fame coach Larry Brown took over a losing Sixers team and had a winning record with the Sixers in each season after the first. He led them to the NBA Championship in 2001 where they were defeated by the Kobe/Shaq Los Angeles Lakers. Brown was named NBA Coach of the Year for 2001.

Philly by the Numbers

_____

Made in the USA
Lexington, KY
25 November 2019

57654835R00204